Praise for
The Grateful Table

A heartening collection. Worthy of quiet reflection and sharing.
—Judy Ford, author of *Every Day Love*

The Grateful Table brings together heartfelt prayers and homilies from a truly diverse group of writers, artists, and visionaries. This is a gracious and unique book that offers a bite-size reflection for every day of the year.
—Billee Sharp, author of *Lemons and Lavender*

The older I get, the more I realize the importance and the power of gratitude. It can help us rise above a situation and be thankful for what we do have instead of focusing on what we don't. I love this book for giving us something to be thankful for every day of the year…not only to begin a meal but also to begin a lifetime of gratitude.
—Allen Klein, author of *The Art of Living Joyfully*

There is nothing quite like the feeling of fellowship that we, as human beings, experience when we come together for the purpose of being thankful for our lives and the many wonderful blessings we share. Every page of *The Grateful Table* gives us the ability to experience that euphoria in a deeply profound and beautiful way.

—David Mezzapelle, author of *Contagious Optimism*

If you've ever thought about starting a daily spiritual practice, but felt you just didn't have enough time, then *The Grateful Table* is just for you. This book gives you the blessings, prayers, and graces that are a perfect daily practice. And since the practice of gratitude is the foundation of a more peaceful and happy life, you will nourish your body, mind, and spirit with every meal you eat.

—Susyn Reeve, author of *The Inspired Life*

In this book of daily blessings, we find a lot to give thanks for. We are reminded that grace is not just for the dinner table. It is an exercise in gratitude, a Thanks Giving that can infuse our meals and our days with appreciation. This beautiful book is in itself a blessing that will inspire you to connect to the grace threading through your life.

—Polly Campbell, author of *Imperfect Spirituality*

My grandparents taught me an old French-Canadian proverb: Anyone who doesn't express their gratitude for all their gifts on a daily basis is a thief. Brenda Knight's new collection reinforces these notions of gratitude, gifts, and daily practice. Keep it on the table and refer to it whenever you are tempted to think you've accomplished everything on your own.

—Phil Cousineau, author of *Burning the Midnight Oil*

Gratitude is at the center of The Code. Sharing a meal with friends and loved ones happens at every single gathering of the Intenders of the Highest Good. Here, fellow Intender Brenda Knight has gathered 365 ways to express thanks for all we are given in this life. *The Grateful Table* is a wonderful tool for manifesting and sharing abundance.

—Tony Burroughs, author of *Get What You Want*

The Grateful Table's anecdotes, meditations and prayers, pulled from poets, philosophers, scientists, rabbis, preachers, Buddhists, rappers, writers, politicians, composers, inventors, and more, help me to understand this eternal flame of love and giving. Knight leads me to a new meditation as a writer: I need to have more gracious characters in novels, a more gracious voice in poems, a more gracious retrospective in nonfiction.

—Nick Belardes, author of *A People's History of the Peculiar*

THE GRATEFUL
TABLE

THE GRATEFUL TABLE

BLESSINGS, PRAYERS AND GRACES
FOR THE DAILY MEAL

BRENDA KNIGHT

FOREWORD BY NINA LESOWITZ

VIVA
EDITIONS

Published in the United States by Viva Editions,
an imprint of Cleis Press Inc., 2246 Sixth Street, Berkeley CA 94710.

Printed in China.
Cover design: Scott Idleman/Blink
Cover illustration: Patrick Morgan/Getty Images
Text design: Frank Wiedemann

First Edition.
10 9 8 7 6 5 4 3 2 1

Hardcover ISBN: 978-1-936740-56-7
E-book ISBN: 978-1-936740-65-9

Library of Congress Cataloging-in-Publication data is available.

ACKNOWLEDGMENTS

The Grateful Table would have never gotten off the ground if not for the singularly ripsniptious Elizabeth Smith. Ashley Shepard and Kara Wuest, editorial aces both, helped make this a "real book." Big thank yous to the team here at Viva, from Cat Snell, who keeps our train on the tracks; to Eva Gantz, promotions wizardess; to birthday bud Sara Giusti, who added major Tupac punch to the mix; to Samantha Kornblum, Virgo marketeer extraordinaire; as well as to Jess LaFrank, poet and bookwallah for the energy and team spirit. Special snaps to Scout, the best office manager and canine-in-chief at any publishing house. I will remain forever grateful to our founders, Frédérique Delacoste and

Felice Newman, for believing in Viva and taking a chance on me.

I also want to thank all the voices in *The Grateful Table* for the beauty of your words and for instilling in others an attitude of gratitude.

CONTENTS

JANUARY · 1

FEBRUARY · 17

MARCH · 35

APRIL · 57

MAY · 75

JUNE · 91

JULY · 109

AUGUST · 125

SEPTEMBER • 141

OCTOBER · 157

november · 173

DECEMBER · 191

FOREWORD

Close your eyes and think about the expression, "giving thanks." Does it bring to mind a Norman Rockwell painting depicting a family with bowed heads and clasped hands? Or do you think about the act of acknowledging a gift or act of kindness? This book aims to take you beyond those expressions of thankfulness and into the realm of transformative change, because saying grace is a key ingredient in living a life full of joy and abundance.

I wasn't raised in a household that said grace, but I was keenly aware from a young age that I had much to be grateful for. Much later, after various travails severely tested that optimism and faith, I began searching for methods, practices, and tools to help me achieve a state of serenity and acceptance. What I discovered led to the writing of *Living Life as a Thank You*, which I coauthored with Mary Beth Sammons in 2009. As it turns out, there is no magic formula or one true spiritual path to discovering what gives life meaning. All it takes is two words—*thank you*—to profoundly change your outlook, and even your life.

No matter your relationship to organized religion, you can add this one ritual to your life, and it will not only increase your appreciation of your food—it will increase the happiness quotient of those you dine with! Research from Harvard Medical School and other institutions shows that happiness is contagious. Happiness—and achieving a state of grace—is not something that you can purchase, wear, or travel to. It is a spiritual experience. And giving thanks is the one true path to happiness.

Many news and magazine articles continue to focus on the importance of the shared meal. It is often the only time we connect with other people who all live busy, full lives. Beyond that, we live in times when it seems like virtually everyone's attention is centered on their digital devices. Beginning the meal with a shared prayer requires your tablemates to turn their attention from far-flung social networks to the bounty in front of them. What a blessing to have a vehicle that enables us to reconnect with our good fortune, and those around us! In *The Grateful Table*, Brenda and I talk about how living a grateful life doesn't come naturally to many people. We need to work intentionally to increase the intensity, duration, and frequency of positive, grateful feelings. This book contains the tools to help you do that with very little effort, and a lot of payoff.

Who wouldn't want to promote healing, harmony, peace, forgiveness, and empowerment in their lives and the lives of their loved ones? Saying thank you before a meal can help you capture those blessings. And with regular practice, expressing appreciation can bring abundance and greater love into your life. As Sri Ramakrishna Paramahamsa said, "The winds of grace blow all the time. All we need to do is set our sails."

Nina Lesowitz

INTRODUCTION

I come from humble circumstances, and for this, I am grateful. My extended family lived on nearby farms in our sylvan part of West Virginia, so there were always aunts and uncles and cousins stopping by with an extra bushel of corn or some freshly canned tomatoes for a sit-down and a nice, long "chin wag." It may have been my great-aunts and uncles, however, who most influenced my childhood mind. To these survivors of the Great War and the Great Depression, even modern conveniences such as ready-baked bread you could buy in a store were the stuff of amazement. They had to grow their own food, bake their own bread, make their own clothes. They were D.I.Y. when it was not fashionable but essential. Aunt Stella and Ida and Uncle Arthur were up with the sun milking cows and tending vegetable patches. Whatever needed doing to keep food on the table and a roof overhead, they did so, and happily. I can imagine my Uncle Delbert's roar of laughter that butchery is now a trendy new hobby undertaken by hipsters in Brooklyn, Portland, San Francisco, and other foodie meccas. I had to help with the sausage-making and I have to agree with my forebears—butchering your own livestock is not glamorous (especially when some were your four-legged farm friends)!

I do think my aunties and uncles would appreciate the recent return to "the homely arts," and not because of any cultural zeitgeist but for this simple reason—what you make with your own hands, you'll appreciate more.

You see, they were grateful for the little things in life—nice weather, good health, an abundant harvest. I feel a sense of pride that my family also did a lot of "inner work" and were fairly accomplished. Aunt Stella was a great dancer and made lace the Etsy crowd would go crazy for. Uncle Wilber was a theologian and great orator—people would come from miles around to hear him preach. Pretty much everybody played piano or organ and all were avid readers who did not bat an eye when I started reading and never stopped. (I even managed to escape a few chores this way by disappearing inside a book and becoming oblivious to all else.)

My elders also said grace at every meal over food they had grown and cooked themselves, sometimes adding a poetic or biblical quote to the mealtime prayer. I learned to be thankful back then on the farm by listening to stories of hard times when folks "did without," a rather stoic all-purpose phrase these Depression-era veterans employed to encompass the lack of food, very little money, no new clothes or shoes, and only hand-me-downs. When I think back to those stories, which seemed mythological to me, they were not complaining. Instead, my elderly relatives related these stories with humor and, surprisingly, gratitude.

I am writing this on Thanksgiving Day, after enjoying a bountiful meal shared with cherished loved ones. And for that, I am filled with gratitude.

I also learned from my dear mother Helen that you only get what you give. I remember well her tithing even when we were having hard times. She would not hear of skipping a week, and I witnessed her do without new things for herself. So, I too will share some of the proceeds from this book to those who might be in need of a helping hand.

A portion of the proceeds from *The Grateful Table* will

go to Building Opportunities for Self-Sufficiency (BOSS). BOSS operates a network of housing and support services in Berkeley, Hayward, and Oakland, California, working directly with at-risk youth and families to help them get back on their feet. Their programs provide whatever level of support people need and request in order to build health, wellness, and self-sufficiency, whether they're seeking one-time assistance or help for longer periods of time.

You can donate to BOSS via their website (www.self-sufficiency.org), or by mailing a check made out to BOSS to 2065 Kittredge St. Ste. E, Berkeley, CA, 94704. All donations are tax deductible.

With true gratitude,
Brenda Knight

january

A New Year for Gratitude

We pray tonight, O God, for confidence in ourselves, our powers and our purposes in this beginning of a New Year. Ward us from all lack of faith and hesitancy and inspire in us not only the determination to do a year's work well, but the unfaltering belief that what we wish to do, we will do. Such Faith, O Lord, is born of Works. Every deed accomplished finishes not only itself but is fallow ground for future deeds. Abundantly endow us, Our Father, with this deed-born Faith.

—W. E. B. Du Bois

Be Kind

Beginning today, treat everyone you meet as if they were going to be dead by midnight. Extend to them all the care, kindness and understanding you can muster, and do it with no thought of any reward. Your life will never be the same again.

—Og Mandino

THE KEY TO A HAPPY LIFE

Gratefulness is the key to a happy life that we hold in our hands, because if we are not grateful, then no matter how much we have we will not be happy, because we will always want to have something else or something more.

—BROTHER DAVID STEINDL-RAST

IN ALL YOUR GLORY

These times of great upheaval are truly gifts unto you. You are constantly surrounded by an environment that is conducive for bringing out your most fulfilling form of expression. Your ego, the part of you that is in service to yourself, is giving way to a much larger, grander you—the you that is in service to others. You are blossoming in all your glory, and it is this blossoming that you have always longed for. Be open, be available, and, in the meantime, be at peace. Your prayers and intentions are all being answered.

—TONY BURROUGHS

FOR THE JOY

5

I Receive ALL of Life with Thanksgiving
I have gratitude for EVERYTHING
that has ever occurred to bring me to this moment.
I give thanks for the joys and the sufferings,
the moments of peace and the flashes of anger,
the compassion and the indifference,
the roar of my courage and the cold sweat of my fear.
I accept gratefully the entirety of my past and my
present life.

—JONATHAN LOCKWOOD HUIE

UNEXPECTED BLESSINGS

6

When we lose one blessing, another is often, most
unexpectedly, given in its place.

—C. S. LEWIS

HOPE

Imagine every day to be the last of a life surrounded
with hopes, cares, anger and fear. The hours that come
unexpectedly will be much the more grateful.

—HORACE

THE TREASURE IS WITHIN

Be at peace with your own soul, then heaven and
earth will be at peace with you. Enter eagerly into
the treasure house that is within you, you will see
the things that are in heaven; for there is but one
single entry into them both. The ladder that leads to
the kingdom is hidden within your soul…dive into
yourself, and into your soul you will discover the stairs
by which to ascend.

—SAINT ISAAC OF NINEVAH

RISE IN GRATITUDE

Keep a pen and a journal next to your bed, and before you rise every morning, make a list of all that you're grateful for, realizing that gratitude will magnetize good things and good people to you. Gratitude also helps us open our hearts for the day.

—RHONDA BYRNE

THE GLADNESS OF THE WORLD

May I reach
That purest heaven, be to other souls
The cup of strength in some great agony,
Enkindle generous ardour, feed pure love,
Beget the smiles that have no cruelty—
Be the sweet presence of a good diffused,
And in diffusion ever more intense.
So shall I join the choir invisible
Whose music is the gladness of the world.

—GEORGE ELIOT

Enjoying the Fruits of Your Labors

This food comes from the Earth and the Sky,
It is the gift of the entire universe
and the fruit of much hard work;
I vow to live a life which is worthy to receive it.

—Grace of the Bodhisattva Buddhists

Look to the Sky

Sometimes I go about pitying myself,
And all the while I am being carried across the sky
by beautiful clouds.

—Ojibwe proverb

All We Have Is Now

We have only this moment, sparkling like a star in our
hand...and melting like a snowflake. Let us use it now
before it is too late.

—Marie Beynon Lyons Ray

Recognizing the Unseen

To Muslims, prayer is a ladder, a journey reaching to heaven. St. Thérèse of Lisieux called it "an uplifting of the heart." In the words of William James, prayer is "the soul and essence of religion," and to Auguste Sabatier, "religion in action." According to the Dakota Sioux physician and author, Ohiyesa, "In the life of the Indian there was only one inevitable duty—the duty of prayer—the daily recognition of the Unseen and Eternal." Mahatma Gandhi practiced a "prayer that needs no speech," and Thomas Merton struggled for a form of prayer in everyday life "with everything I touch." For Brother David Steindl-Rast, "Prayer is unlimited mindfulness."

—Phil Cousineau

14

Changing Seasons of Life

If we had no winter, the spring would not be so pleasant. If we did not sometimes taste of adversity, prosperity would not be so welcome.

—Anne Bradstreet

15

BE HERE NOW

No longer forward nor behind
I look in hope or fear;
But, grateful, take the good I find,
The best of now and here.

—JOHN GREENLEAF WHITTIER

YOU HAVE ALL YOU NEED

Gratitude unlocks the fullness of life. It turns what
we have into enough, and more. It turns denial into
acceptance, chaos into order, and confusion into clarity.
It turns problems into gifts, failures into successes,
the unexpected into perfect timing, and mistakes
into important events. Gratitude makes sense of our
past, brings peace for today, and creates a vision for
tomorrow.

—MELODY BEATTIE

Food for the Soul

18

Salutations!
O Merciful God
Who provides food for the body and soul,
You who have kindly granted what is spread before us.
We thank you.
Bless the loving hands that prepared this meal and us
who are to enjoy it, please.
Homage, homage,
Homage to thee!

—Tamil prayer

Be a Candle

19

There are two ways of spreading light: to be the candle
or the mirror that reflects it.

—Edith Wharton

Surround Yourself with Gratitude

It's no secret that practicing gratitude as a daily ritual rewires your brain to see the cup half full. You'll be happier, healthier, and more grateful for the blessings in your life.

Have you ever noticed the way it feels to be around grateful people? You feel energized, alive, and inspired to give thanks yourself for the friends, families, and community members that make a difference in your daily living. When we're grateful, we reach out to help others in need, instead of focusing on our own woes, anger, or resentments.

—Nina Lesowitz

Be of Service

Make a list of your skills, talents, gifts, and abilities and a list of causes you believe in and want to support. Choose what you would like to offer and where you'd like to offer it; then take action to explore where and how you can best be of service.

—Polly Campbell

EVERY DAY SUCCEED

Gratitude is the intention to count your blessings every day, every minute, while avoiding, whenever possible, the belief that you need or deserve different circumstances.

—TIMOTHY RAY MILLER

THE ABUNDANCE OF BEING

When you are grateful, fear disappears and abundance appears.

—ANTHONY ROBBINS

A LIGHT WITHIN

Plato said more than 2,500 years ago, "A grateful mind
is a great mind which eventually attracts to itself great
things." A tremendous insight! The grateful person
is great because he or she has turned on all the lights
within. You may say of someone, "He has so much,
and he is so grateful." But by Plato's law, it may be that
he has so much because he is so grateful. The grateful
heart actually opens the way to the flow and becomes an
attractive force to draw to itself great things.

—ERIC BUTTERWORTH

BE OPEN

Something opens our wings.
Something makes boredom and hurt disappear.
Someone fills the cup in front of us.
We taste only sacredness.

—RUMI

The Little Things in Life

Give thanks for a little and you will find a lot.

—Hausa proverb

Tomorrow's Joy

Start your day with this intention: Today I will be grateful. I will start the process of turning today's pain into tomorrow's joy.

—Melody Beattie

Life's Simple Rituals

Anytime someone has a kind of ritual in their lives— which is a particular, deliberate choice of routine—it's beautiful to me. It's nice to have a way to think about it, and eating a certain way brings that ritual and meaning to an aspect of my life.

—Jonathan Safran Foer

PAUSING TO APPRECIATE

Whatever our individual troubles and challenges may be, it's important to pause every now and then to appreciate all that we have, on every level. We need to literally "count our blessings," give thanks for them, allow ourselves to enjoy them, and relish the experience of prosperity we already have.

—SHAKTI GAWAIN

29

ALL WE RECEIVE FROM OTHERS

When we become more fully aware that our success is due in large measure to the loyalty, helpfulness, and encouragement we have received from others, our desire grows to pass on similar gifts. Gratitude spurs us on to prove ourselves worthy of what others have done for us. The spirit of gratitude is a powerful energizer.

—WILFERD A. PETERSON

30

Heaven on Earth

Both abundance and lack exist simultaneously in our lives, as parallel realities. It is always our conscious choice which secret garden we will tend…when we choose not to focus on what is missing from our lives but are grateful for the abundance that's present—love, health, family, friends, work, the joys of nature and personal pursuits that bring us pleasure—the wasteland of illusion falls away and we experience Heaven on earth.

—Sarah Ban Breathnach

february

REMEMBER TO GIVE THANKS

All this is God,
right here in my pea-green house
each morning
and I mean,
though often forget,
to give thanks…

—ANNE SEXTON

THE FULLNESS OF LIFE

Gratefulness—the simple response of our heart to this
life in all its fullness—goes beyond boundaries of creed,
age, vocation, gender, and nation.

—J. ROBERT MOSKIN

SOWING CLOVER

In the dark of the moon, in the flying snow; in the dead of winter, war spreading, families dying, the world in danger, I walk the rocky hillside, sowing clover.

—WENDELL BERRY

LOOK FOR THE GOOD

Gratitude should not be just a reaction to getting what you want, but an all-the-time gratitude, the kind where you notice the little things and where you constantly look for the good, even in unpleasant situations.
Start bringing gratitude to your experiences, instead of waiting for a positive experience in order to feel grateful.

—MARELISA FÁBREGA

Just Enjoy

Those who allow their day to pass by without practicing
generosity and enjoying life's pleasures are like
blacksmith's bellows: they breathe but do not live.

—Sanskrit proverb

Never Be Less

May the abundance of this table never fail
And never be less, thanks to the blessings of God,
Who has fed us and satisfied our needs.
To him be the glory for ever. Amen.

In peace let us eat this food
Which the Lord hath provided for us.
Blessed be the Lord in His gifts. Amen.

Glory be to the Father, and to the Son,
And to the Holy Ghost, now and always,
World without end. Amen.

—Armenian grace

CONNECTED TO THE DIVINE

True abundance is not about gathering more things, it's about touching the place in us that is connected to the divine source of abundance, so that we know what we need in the moment will be provided.

—MARY MANIN MORRISSEY

SLOWING DOWN TO SAVOR LIFE

Let us not get so busy or live so fast that we can't listen to the music of the meadow or the symphony that glorifies the forest. Some things in the world are far more important than wealth; one of them is the ability to enjoy simple things.

—DALE CARNEGIE

GRATEFUL, NO MATTER WHAT

A thankful person is thankful under all circumstances. A complaining soul complains even if he lives in paradise.

—BAHA'U'LLAH

BRIGHT AS DAY

Last night, when I walked the dog, here in Wisconsin, it was minus 15 degrees—minus 26 with the wind chill, according to the weather site…having said that, even walking last night in minus 26, the air was so preternaturally clear, the moon was actually doing that "shining bright as day" thing, the shadows just fell perfectly to the snow, and the stars looked like they'd been draped by a Hollywood set designer. The beauty, even as my skin—where it was exposed to the cold air— actually hurt, was still so overwhelming and so peaceful. That's a blessing.

—NEIL GAIMAN

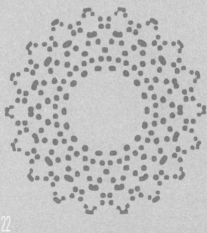

Conscious Gratitude

You simply will not be the same person two months from now after consciously giving thanks each day for the abundance that exists in your life. And you will have set in motion an ancient spiritual law: the more you have and are grateful for, the more will be given you.

—Sarah Ban Breathnach

Keeping Track of Blessings

Hem your blessings with thankfulness so they don't unravel.

—Anonymous

THE FOOD ON THE TABLE

He left it for us.
Something that should be for the people's happiness.
They will be strong in body from it.
He left us all this food.
He scattered this all over the Earth.
Now we will give one thanks.
That he has left us all this food to live on.
On this Earth.
This is the way it should be in our minds.

—SENECA INDIAN THANKS-GIVING PRAYER

LOVE LOCKDOWN

Show some gratitude, leave the attitude at home.

—KANYE WEST

Consider the Ineffable

We are all spiritual creatures and live spiritual existences, however confused and disguised and sometimes downtrodden these lives might sometimes feel. But this is why we can be so profoundly moved by certain experiences and certain art, why millions of people can be moved by a sequence of notes written by Mozart or Beethoven or Elgar. Why does that series of notes move us? It resonates with something inside of us that is beyond explanation. It is ineffable. That is spirituality. That is what connects us all. That is why it is important to me to do what I do, to be a storyteller. Because telling stories heals us, doesn't it?

—Sir Ben Kingsley

Good Days

What good is the warmth of summer, without the cold of winter to give it sweetness.

—John Steinbeck

JUST ONE THING

17

To all else thou hast given us, O Lord,
we ask for but one thing more:
Give us
grateful hearts.

—George Herbert

PURE DELIGHT

18

Only when your consciousness is totally focused on
the moment you are in can you receive whatever gift,
lesson, or delight that moment has to offer.

—Barbara De Angelis

GIVE US THIS DAY

One more day to serve.
One more hour to love.
One more minute to praise.
For this day I am grateful.
If I awaken to the morning sun,
I am grateful.

—MARY LOU KOWNACKI

SHARING

Silent gratitude isn't very much use to anyone.

—GERTRUDE STEIN

19

20

Asking the Big Questions

21

Take out your journal and a pen and set aside twenty minutes for this exercise in thankfulness.

Gratitude is the surest way to heal your heart and soul and to move your focus to what is good and working in your life. It's also the fastest way, I've found, to make a difference in your day. When we commit to a regular gratitude practice, we start to see the webs of meaning sticking to all the crannies in our lives and we find even more reasons to be grateful for all that we have.

For example, when I lost four magazine assignments, and all of my income, in a twenty-four-hour period, I got nervous, then I freaked. Then, after a few deep breaths, I got curious and started asking The Big Questions: What is the meaning behind this? What can I do with this? What is working?

The answers to those questions helped me to get clear about my situation and helped me to recognize all that I did have to be grateful for (a husband with a job, a little money in the bank, breath in my lungs, and mint chocolate chip in the freezer).

From that place of gratitude, I could start seeing the possibilities the lost work provided. It freed up

my schedule to follow a dream I'd had for decades—
writing *Imperfect Spirituality*. When I gave thanks for
my life as it was, I could see the meaning behind the
lost assignments, and a dismal situation became a life-
changing experience.

Now, you try it. In this exercise you'll have a chance
to begin a practice of gratitude and find those gifts of
meaning in your own life.

1. List ten things you are thankful for.
2. How many of those things evolved out of less than
   perfect circumstances?
3. Pick one to write about. Describe how it came to be
   in your life.
4. What did you learn from it?
5. What did you do as a result of it?
6. What meaning does it hold for you?

—Polly Campbell

THE WORLD IS WHAT YOU ARE

22 The world is a great mirror. It reflects back to you what you are. If you are loving, if you are friendly, if you are helpful, the world will prove loving and friendly and helpful to you. The world is what you are.

—THOMAS DREIER

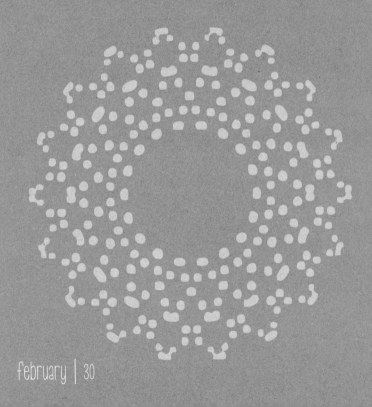

In Appreciation

23

What if you gave someone a gift, and they neglected to thank you for it—would you be likely to give them another? Life is the same way. In order to attract more of the blessings that life has to offer, you must truly appreciate what you already have.

—Ralph Marston

You Get What You Give

The blessings we evoke for another descend upon ourselves.

—Edmund Gibson

24

Each morning, at the thought of the effort that I must expend to fully be myself and feel completely alive, my body tires and heart balks, the mind protests and ingrained self-defeating patterns flare up, promising old, familiar rewards of illusory safety and the numbness of thwarted growth.

Only my spirit stands apart from these deceptions and, gently whispering, beckons me to the place of magical possibility.

Each morning, I follow. I know that I awake the same person who I was before I ever undertook becoming the person I truly am. And so I rise and choose not to revisit my well-furnished rut but dare to advance, through conscious, principled, and disciplined actions, into mystery and the unknown, where the person I am already exists, waiting to be claimed.

I think of myself as a journeyman with a portable spiritual tool kit. In the old days, the journeyman carpenter or housebuilder was willing to travel in any

direction to provide his services, so long as the trip did
not require more than 24 hours of travel.

For me, each 24 hour day is a journey I set forth,
bearing my spiritual tools. For those hours, I will seek
to be of service and to practice gratitude in the world
that I encounter.

—ALAN KAUFMAN

OUR LIFE JOURNEYS

Praise the bridge that carried you over.

—GEORGE COLMAN

DO THE MATH

The hardest arithmetic to master is that which enables
us to count our blessings.

—ERIC HOFFER

This Great Big Beautiful World

You know, there's a lot more to life than meets the eye. It's a great big beautiful world. Bliss is our nature. Life is beautiful. It's all there. It's all possible. I'm grateful for *that*, buster!

—David Lynch

To Boldly Go

Live long and prosper.

—Leonard Nimoy

march

LIVING ALOHA

Get acquainted with the power of simple goodness, as illustrated by the Hawaiian island tradition of "Living Aloha," which is the Native Islanders' way of daily living—simple acts of goodness every day. When at the grocery store, return the cart, and help the elderly man struggling with his bags. Open doors for people; say, "Hello," with a smile. Every day and in every way choose to take the high road in your travels. The view is much more beautiful up top!

—BRENDA KNIGHT

LIFE IS SO RICH

In ordinary life, we hardly realize that we receive a good deal more than we give, and that it is only with gratitude that life becomes rich.

—DIETRICH BONHOEFFER

UNEXPECTED TEACHERS

Being thankful changes our energy from demanding to appreciation. Instead of increasing our expectations of how things should be, we can move toward recognizing what is. I like learning from my pets—every caring gesture or morsel of food is appreciated. It's important to stay in touch with the reality of how much we've been given!

—DOROTHEA HOVER-KRAMER

3

GROWING MORE GRATEFUL

The word "miracle" aptly describes a seed.

—JACK KRAMER

4

ONE GOOD DAY

5

I reverently speak in the presence of the Great Parent
God: I give Thee grateful thanks that Thou hast enabled
me to live this day, the whole day, in obedience to the
excellent spirit of Thy ways.

—SHINTO EVENING PRAYER

JOY, LOVE, AND BLISS

6

Softness, and peace, and joy, and love, and bliss,
Exalted Manna, gladness of the best,
Heaven in ordinary, man well drest,
The milky way, the bird of Paradise,
Church-bells beyond the stars heard, the soul's blood,
The land of spices; something understood.

—GEORGE HERBERT

CRYSTAL CLARITY

What I really want to say is that, astonishingly, the reward for truth, after all this way, is not justice or knowledge or expertise—though these things may happen—but joy, and the reward for kindness is not goodness or being thought well of or even having kindness returned—though these things may happen too. No, the reward for kindness, as well, is joy.

—MARK NEPO

THE OLD AND THE NEW

I awoke this morning with devout thanksgiving for my friends, the old and the new.

—RALPH WALDO EMERSON

GOOD HABITS

9

The Christian writer G.K. Chesterton has the right idea when he said we need to get in the habit of "taking things with gratitude and not taking things for granted." Write a letter to your relatives acknowledging the special role a relative who is now gone has played in your family circle. Ask them to say a prayer of thanksgiving for this person and the legacy he or she has left for all of you.

—NINA LESOWITZ

CHOICES

10

There are only two ways to live your life. One is as though nothing is a miracle. The other is as though everything is a miracle.

—ALBERT EINSTEIN

LIVING THE GOOD LIFE

In our grandparents' day, there was a pride and pleasure in such resourcefulness. In my case, both sets of grandparents grew all kinds of food in their gardens; I also heard tales of them raising rabbits and chickens during WWII. I remember the big basket that my grandmother would fill with potatoes from her modest garden, and I vividly remember standing in the fragrant thicket at the back of the gooseberry bushes in my father's parents' garden, sneaking a few of the sour fruits in the leafy shade. Their houses rarely changed through the years, but when something new arrived, even a tablecloth, we'd inspect and compliment it. How pretty! What beautiful quality! What a bargain! They valued their achievements and took little for granted. I aspire to the same.

—BILLEE SHARP

A Whole in Every Part

Even at prayer, our eyes look inward;
If the gate to the holy is shut, we just turn away.

The One is only the One, everyone knows—
What mirroring icon could hold it face to face?

Held back unnoticed, grief bruises the heart;
Not reaching the river, a raindrop is swallowed by dust.

If a story brings only tears and not blood to the eyes,
It is only a lovers' tale.

Whoever can't see the whole in every part plays at blind
man's bluff;

A wise man tastes the Tigris in every sip.

—Ghalib

BE A GOOD IN THE WORLD

But I have found that in the simple act of living with hope, and in the daily effort to have a positive impact in the world, the days I do have are made all the more meaningful and precious. And for that I am grateful.

—ELIZABETH EDWARDS

SPARKING THE INNER FLAME

Sometimes we feel deflated, or overwhelmed, or someone or something hurts us, disappoints us, or we hear bad news about a loved one's medical condition. On those days, when you feel your light has gone out, remember there is always a glimmer of hope and something to be thankful for. Sometimes our light goes out, but is blown again into instant flame by an encounter with another human being. Each of us owes the deepest thanks to those who have rekindled this inner light.

—ALBERT SCHWEITZER

14

GIFTS FROM GOD

15

Start living now. Stop saving the good china for that special occasion. Stop withholding your love until that special person materializes. Every day you are alive is a special occasion. Every minute, every breath, is a gift from God.

—MARY MANIN MORRISSEY

INNER WORK

16

Happiness depends more on the inward disposition of mind than on outward circumstances.

—BENJAMIN FRANKLIN

THE SERENITY OF THE STARS

I arise this day
With love in my heart,
Through the warmth of the sun,
The radiance of the moon,
Freedom of the wind,
Joy of rushing water,
Splendor of fire,
Stability of earth,
Serenity of stars, and
The wisdom of silence.
I embrace this day
Through the grace of life to guide me
And the promise of love to inspire me.

—IRISH PRAYER

SHARE THE LOVE

Happiness is not so much in having as sharing. We make a living by what we get, but we make a life by what we give.

—NORMAN MACEWEN

MAY THERE BE FOOD FOR ALL

Let us give thanks
For the food we are about to eat.
May there be food for all,
Abundant and healthful.
Let us have the wisdom to choose to eat only that
Which enhances our precious energy
And sustains us through our labors and rest.

—Adapted from *An Haggadah of Liberation*

PLANTING SEEDS

All the flowers of all the tomorrows are in the seeds of today.

—Indian proverb

GOOD COMPANY

I have perceiv'd that to be with
those I like is enough,
To stop in company with the rest
at evening is enough,
To be surrounded by beautiful, curious, breathing,
Laughing flesh is enough…

—WALT WHITMAN

How We Grow

Be thankful that you don't already have everything you desire. If you did, what would there be to look forward to?

Be thankful when you don't know something
For it gives you the opportunity to learn.

Be thankful for the difficult times.
During those times you grow.

Be thankful for your limitations
Because they give you opportunities for improvement.

Be thankful for each new challenge
Because it will build your strength and character.

Be thankful for your mistakes
They will teach you valuable lessons.

Be thankful when you're tired and weary
Because it means you've made a difference.

It is easy to be thankful for the good things.
A life of rich fulfillment comes to those who are
also thankful for the setbacks.

GRATITUDE can turn a negative into a positive.

Find a way to be thankful for your troubles
and they can become your blessings.

—ANONYMOUS

BECOMING LIGHT

The burden which is well borne becomes light.

—OVID

23

LOVE, GRACE, AND GRATITUDE

Happiness cannot be traveled to, owned, earned, worn
or consumed. Happiness is a spiritual experience of
living every minute with love, grace and gratitude.

—DENIS WAITLEY

24

Your Lucky Stars

25

We can thank our lucky stars when once in a blue moon we find rare and kindred souls along the pathway of our lives.

—Laurel Burch

Origins of Abundance

26

Within the context of everything you do, pause—really slow down—and say thank you. Look the checker in the eye, take a breath, and say, "thank you." Pause before a meal and give thanks to the farmers and the Earth and the animals or the Coca-Cola distributor who brought the food to your table. Say, "thank you."

—Polly Campbell

WE ARE ROSES

We wouldn't ask why a rose that grew from the concrete for having damaged petals; in turn, we would all celebrate its tenacity, we would all love its will to reach the sun. Well, we are the roses: this is the concrete and these are my damaged petals, don't ask me why. Thank God, and ask me how.

—TUPAC SHAKUR

27

Every Glass is Half Full (at Least)

28

Hardship often plays a significant role in birthing gratitude. There is a tension between wallowing in self-pity and turning that energy into tools of giving and gratitude—the whole glass half-full concept.

When brokenness and suffering enter our lives, we have a choice whether to let them simmer and stew, depleting our sense of peace, faith, and hope for healing and love.

That is the time when we have to be purposeful about bringing fresh ideas and perspectives, along with a greater sense of possibility, in place of the weariness sinking into our broken places.

—Mary Beth Sammons

Life Is a Miracle

Miracles, in the sense of phenomena we cannot explain, surround us on every hand: life itself is the miracle of miracles.

29

—George Bernard Shaw

Giving Voice to Gratitude

In the end, though, maybe we must all give up trying to pay back the people in this world who sustain our lives. In the end, maybe it's wiser to surrender before the miraculous scope of human generosity and to just keep saying thank you, forever and sincerely, for as long as we have voices.

30

—Elizabeth Gilbert

"Any day I'm vertical is a good day"
—that's what I always say.
And I give thanks
that I am healthy.
If you ask me,
"How are you?"
I'll answer, "GREAT!"
because in saying so,
I make it so.
And I give thanks
that I can choose my attitude.
When Life gives me dark clouds and rain,
I appreciate the moisture
which brings a soft curl to my hair.
When Life gives me sunshine,
I gratefully turn my face up
to feel its warmth on my cheeks.
When Life brings fog,
I hug my sweater around me
and give thanks for the cool shroud of mystery
that makes the familiar seem different and intriguing.
When Life brings snow,

31

I dash outside to catch the first flakes on my tongue,
relishing the icy miracle that is a snowflake.
Life's events and experiences
are like the weather—
they come and go,
no matter what my preference.
So, what the heck?!
I might as well decide to enjoy them.
For indeed,
there IS a time for every purpose
under Heaven.
Each season brings its own unique blessings.
And I give thanks.

—BJ GALLAGHER

april

GOD IS (VERY) GOOD

To be grateful is to recognize the Love of God in everything He has given us—and He has given us everything. Every breath we draw is a gift of His love, every moment of existence is a grace, for it brings with it immense graces from Him.

Gratitude therefore takes nothing for granted, is never unresponsive, is constantly awakening to new wonder and to praise of the goodness of God. For the grateful person knows that God is good, not by hearsay but by experience. And that is what makes all the difference.

—THOMAS MERTON

THE WATER OF LIFE

Many a man curses the rain that falls upon his head, and knows not that it brings abundance to drive away the hunger.

—SAINT BASIL

GROW YOUR OWN

There are many ways of learning to love, not only yourself, but those around you, as well. Another is to plant and grow some food of your own. Most people don't realize it, but something very special happens when we nurture and consume food that we have grown for ourselves. Not only does the life force in it transfer to us when we eat it, the love that we put into caring for it has a magical way of returning to us from Mother Earth herself. Indeed, she befriends all those who care for the least of her creatures.

And it doesn't matter whether it's an acre of organic gardens you're growing or a single kumquat tree or tomato plant you keep on the patio. It can even be a batch of sprouts (for those who want the quickest results) that live on your kitchen windowsill. Regardless of what you plant, you will have shortened the gap between you and your food supply by being just that much less reliant on someone else to provide you with your food. It is a subtle shift, but one that raises your Spirit the minute you cover the little seeds over with soil and water them.

—Tony Burroughs

Live Beautifully

4

Well, you're beautiful. Go out and live like it.

—Bill Clinton

A Grateful Heart

5

A sense of blessedness comes from a change of heart, not from more blessings.

—Mason Cooley

THE HARVEST'S YIELD

Wheresoe'er I turn mine eyes
Around on earth or toward the skies,
I see Thee in the starry field,
I see Thee in the harvest's yield,
In every breath, in every sound,
An echo of thy name is found.
The blade of grass, the simple flower,
Bear witness to Thy matchless pow'r.
My every thought, Eternal God of Heaven,
Ascends to Thee, to who all praise be given.

—ABRAHAM IBN EZRA

MAKING THE MOST OF IT

I make the most of all that comes and the least of
all that goes.

—SARA TEASDALE

Peace in Every Bite

This plate is filled with food.
I am aware that each morsel is the fruit of much hard work
By those who produced it.

—Thich Nhat Hanh

Exultation of Larks

Birds sing after a storm; why shouldn't people feel as free
to delight in whatever sunlight remains to them?

—Rose Fitzgerald Kennedy

Truth and Beauty

Life is full of beauty. Notice it. Notice the bumblebee,
the small child, and the smiling faces. Smell the rain,
and feel the wind. Live your life to the fullest potential,
and fight for your dreams.

—Ashley Smith

Song of Songs

But happiness floats.
It doesn't need you to hold it down.
It doesn't need anything.
Happiness lands on the roof of the next house,
Singing...

—Naomi Shihab Nye

Rejoice!

This is the day which the Lord has made. Let us rejoice
and be glad in it.

—Psalm 118:24

What Mother Earth Has Given

May we walk with grace
and may the light of the universe
shine upon our path.

—Anonymous

RITES OF SPRING

One of the daintiest joys of spring is the falling of soft rain among blossoms.

—MARY WEBB

MAY THIS BE A DAY OF JOY

Money may be the husk of many things, but not the kernel. It brings you food, but not appetite; medicine, but not health; acquaintances, but not friends; servants, but not loyalty; days of joy, but not peace or happiness.

—HENRIK IBSEN

How Can I Help?

What is a Friend? When a friend says, "I need you!" what do you say?

Do you say, "What happened?" or do you say, "How can I help?"

Does it really matter what happened—or does it matter only that your friend needs you, and has asked for your help?

God never asks us—"What happened?"

He says: "I love you—I am your friend!"

—Nina Lesowitz

Random Acts of Kindness

Whoever you are—I have always depended on the kindness of strangers.

—Tennessee Williams

BALANCING ACT

18

We also deem those happy, who from the experience of
life, have learned to bear its ills and without descanting
on their weight.

—JUVENAL

QUIET MIND

19

Surely there is something in the unruffled calm of
nature that overawes our little anxieties and doubts; the
sight of the deep-blue sky and the clustering stars above
seems to impart a quiet to the mind.

—JONATHAN EDWARDS

BY THE LIGHT OF THE MOON

20

As the moon brings sun to those turned from the light,
the opened heart brings love to those struggling through
darkness. It is important to remember here that the
moon is not the source of light but a reflection...

—MARK NEPO

BE BIGGER

Life is a series of experiences, each one of which makes us bigger, even though sometimes it is hard to realize this. For the world was built to develop character, and we must learn that the setbacks and grieves which we endure help us in our marching onward.

—HENRY FORD

ALL WE NEED IS LOVE

I will not wait to love as best as I can. We thought we were young and that there would be time to love well sometime in the future. This is a terrible way to think. It is no way to live, to wait to love.

—DAVE EGGERS

FOOD FOR THE SOUL

Flowers are sunshine, food, and medicine to the soul.

—LUTHER BURBANK

CULTIVATING YOUR DIGNITY

24

There is as much dignity in tilling a field as in writing a poem.

—BOOKER T. WASHINGTON

DOMO ARIGATO

A globetrotting friend of mine told me that the first thing she would do before setting foot in another country was learn how to say, "Thank you," in the native tongue. "You'd be surprised at the delight others take in hearing a foreigner's tongue speak their own language," she said. "They were sometimes surprised, other times impressed, and sometimes they would have no idea what I was saying! But they were always grateful for my attempts."

Here's a list of the world's many ways to express your gratitude:

25

Arabic: Shukran
Czech: D kuji
Danish: Tak

Dutch: Dank u
Estonian: Tänan teid
Filipino: Salamat
Finnish: Kiitos
French: Merci
Gaelic: Go raibh maith agat
German: Danke
Hungarian: Köszönöm
Indonesian: Terima kasih
Italian: Grazie
Japanese: Arigato
Latvian: Paldies
Norwegian: Takk
Polish: Dzi kuj
Portuguese: Obrigado
Romanian: Mul umesc
Spanish: Gracias
Swahili: Asante
Swedish: Tack
Vietnamese: Cảm ơn bạn
Welsh: Diolch yn fawr

—Brenda Knight

Wow, Life Is Good

Good food is an amazing blessing. Whenever you
can sit down to a table and eat food that is extremely
delicious, and you are surrounded by people you love,
and you enjoy every flavor and every bite, it's, "Wow,
life is good." You can't truly grow until you can fully
appreciate a good meal.

—Alicia Keys

Release the Divine

By saying grace, we release the Divine sparks in our
food.

—Rabbi Herschel Schachter

Full of splendor and beauty
Full of life.
Of Souls Hidden,
Of treasures of the Holy Spirit,
Fountains of strength,
Of greatness and beauty.
Proudly I ascend
Toward the heights of the World Soul
That gives life to the universe.
How majestic the vision
Come, enjoy,
Come, find peace,
Embrace delight,
Taste and see that God is good.
Why spend your substance on what does not nourish
And your labor on what cannot satisfy?
Listen to me, and you will enjoy what is good,
And find delight in what is truly precious.

—ABRAHAM ISAAC KOOK

Pass It On

29

You have it easily in your power to increase the sum
total of the world's happiness now. How? By giving a
few words of sincere appreciation to someone who is
lonely or discouraged. Perhaps you will forget tomorrow
the kind words you say today, but the recipient may
cherish them over a lifetime.

—Dale Carnegie

Say Grace

It's interesting how some of us are so readily inclined
to see the dark side of things, even when we are
surrounded by extraordinary beauty. We complain
out of habit, thinking, often unconsciously, that
we'll receive some nice reward for all our grumbling.
Unfortunately, we may get our treat, but we will also
have to live out the results of our complaining, and thus
miss out on some of the greatest gifts Mother Earth
has to offer. Or it's when we hold our attention on
her beauty, that something special is called up within
us; something that instinctively makes us want to take

30

good care of the Earth. From that point on, we clearly see where our greatest rewards are coming from. They come from taking care of that which is taking care of us.

—TONY BURROUGHS

may

FLOWER POWER

The earth laughs in flowers.

—RALPH WALDO EMERSON

SONGS OF LOVE

God, we thank you for all your gifts.
This day, this night,
These fruits, these flowers,
These trees, these waters—
With all these treasures you have endowed us.
The heat of the sun, the light of the moon,
The songs of the birds and the coolness of the breeze,
The green, green grass like a mattress of velvet,
All owe their existence to your grace.
Dear God,
May we forever breathe the breath of your love
And every moment be aware
of your presence above.

—PAKISTANI PRAYER

ONLY CONNECT

Let us be grateful to the people who make us happy—they are the charming gardeners who make our souls blossom.

—MARCEL PROUST

ATTITUDE OF GRATITUDE

When a person doesn't have gratitude, something is missing in his or her humanity.

—ELIE WIESEL

BE AS A LITTLE CHILD

Judge nothing, you will be happy. Forgive everything, you will be happier. Love everything, you will be happiest.

—SRI CHINMOY

GRACIOUSNESS

Hospitality is all about graciously giving and taking. It's not about impressing people or overwhelming them with your cleverness or skill. It's simply sharing what you have and taking what is offered. The greatest hospitality I've ever been shown is when I invited someone to my house for dinner without knowing they were vegetarian. They ate the food that was offered with nothing but a heartfelt "thank you." And baby, it was ribs.

—ALTON BROWN

NEVER FORGET

We've made life a battlefield when it should be a playground. It's all about beauty, wonder, mystery…but we forget that, and almost purposefully. We must have a more mindful attitude. Be mindful of your breath. Be mindful of your body sensations. Be mindful of your choices. These are good ways to actually know your experiences, to remember to play and be alive.

—DEEPAK CHOPRA

Thanks, Mom!

All that I have comes from my Mother!
I give myself over to this pot.
My thoughts are on the good,
the healing properties of this food.
My hands are balanced, I season well!

I give myself over to this pot.
Life is being given to me.
I commit to sharing, I feed others.
I feed She Who Feeds Me.

I give myself over to this gift.
I adorn this table with food.
I invite lovers and friends to come share.
I thank you for this gift.
All that I have comes from my Mother!

—Luisah Teish

LUCKY IN LIFE

9

Property is for the comfort of life, not for the accumulation of wealth. A sage, having been asked who is lucky and who is not, replied: "He is lucky who has eaten and sowed, but he is unlucky who has died and not enjoyed."

—SA'DI

BREAD IS LOVE

10

So often bread is taken for granted,
Yet there is so much of beauty in bread—
Beauty of the sun and the soil,
Beauty of human toil.
Winds and rains have caressed it,
Christ, Himself, blessed it.

—CHRISTIAN PRAYER

BLESSED BE

Blessed are those who give without remembering. And blessed are those who take without forgetting.

—BERNARD MELTZER

SUNNY DAYS

Keep your face always toward the sunshine—and shadows will fall behind you.

—WALT WHITMAN

BE GLAD

I am grateful for my family and friends,
a job to earn my keep, and the health to do it,
and opportunities and the lessons I've learned.
Let me never lose sight of the simple blessings
that form the fabric and foundation of my life.
I am blessed, yesterday, today and tomorrow.

—ABBY WILLOWROOT

JUST ONE MOMENT

God gave you a gift of 86,400 seconds today. Have you used one to say "Thank you?"

—WILLIAM A. WARD

KIND WORDS

God's pleasures are simple ones; health, the rapture of a May morning, sunshine, kind words, benevolent acts, the glow of good-humor.

—F. W. ROBERTSON

BE INSPIRING

You never take life for granted. You never receive possibilities lightly. The opportunity is always there to help somebody. We all need help remaining in touch with our spirit and finding our own voice and locating inspiration.

—ALICIA KEYS

Take a Deep Breath

Problems do not seem as overwhelming when you take
a few moments to count your blessings and appreciate
what exists in your life. Emotionally, gratitude is the
equivalent of taking a deep breath and relaxing.

Research shows that people who actively practice
appreciation and gratitude in their lives are happier.
The expression of gratitude is a feeling, a sense of awe,
wonder, and appreciation for what you have and what is
around you.

—Susyn Reeve

Love Is Everywhere

Nature is too thin a screen; the glory of the omnipresent
God bursts through everywhere.

—Ralph Waldo Emerson

SHEER JOY

When you rise in the morning,
Give thanks for the light, for your life, for your strength.
Give thanks for your food and for the joy of living.
If you see no reason to give thanks,
The fault lies in yourself.

—TECUMSEH

ILLUMINATION

The success of my first book, *Everything Is Illuminated,*
allowed me at a very early age to have control of my
time and my purpose, and all but guaranteed that
I would have a second book published—which is
something I never remotely took for granted. I was an
author all of a sudden. And it felt really good. I hope
I would have been just as grateful for the *experience* of
writing the book even if it had been utterly trashed or
ignored.

—JONATHAN SAFRAN FOER

IMPONDERABLES

How beautiful and perfect are the animals! How perfect is
my soul!

How perfect the earth, and the minutest thing upon it!

What is called good is perfect, and what is called bad is just
as perfect,

The vegetables and minerals are all perfect, and the
imponderable fluids are perfect;

Slowly and surely they have passed on to this, and slowly
and surely they yet pass on...

I swear I think there is nothing but immortality!

—WALT WHITMAN

SETTING THE TABLE

I'd rather have roses on my table than diamonds on
my neck.

—EMMA GOLDMAN

To Be of Use

23

God gave man work, not to burden him, but to bless him, and useful work, willingly, cheerfully, effectively done, has always been the finest expression of the human spirit.

—Walter R. Courtenay

No Worries

24

There is only one way to happiness, and that is to cease worrying about things which are beyond the power of our will.

—Epictetus

SECOND CHANCES

We give thanks for all those times we have arisen from the depths or simply taken a tiny step toward something new. May we be empowered by extraordinary second chances. And as we enter the world anew, let us turn the tides of despair into endless waves of hope.

—MOLLY FUMIA

25

AWARENESS

He who knows that enough is enough will always have enough.

—LAO TZU

26

PLANTING BLESSINGS

27

I spent my summers on my grandparents' farm in Texas, and my grandfather, in particular, taught me so much. He put a seed in the palm of my hand once and didn't say much about it. But I came to see the blessing of what a seed is, what it takes to be nurtured, to plant it, to protect it, to keep it in harmony with the elements, with the sun, the vermin, and to help it to realize its deep space of potentiality. My grandfather taught me all of that, without ever saying much. I think that lesson has informed everything about me.

—FOREST WHITAKER

ENCOURAGING WORDS

Tonight we give thanks for the great gift of friendship
and in particular for my great friend...thank you for the
circumstances that brought us together and have bound us
together into the sacred bundle of life. Thank you also for
the gift of our friendship: for knowledge that comforts,
for words that encourage, for insight that blesses, for all
the experience shared, for the sweet bliss of knowing each
other deeply in so many ways; for history and a hope of the
future, for conversation and laughter, for silence, for bearing
each other's witness truly, for holding each other safe in our
hearts with great love and tenderness.

—DAPHNE ROSE KINGMA

ONE SMILE IS WORTH A THOUSAND

Thank you for the reflection of Your Smile in all we see.

—KENNETH KURTZ

Lilacs and Love

In the door-yard fronting an old farm-house, near the
white-wash'd palings,

Stands the lilac bush, tall-growing, with heart-shaped
leaves of rich green,

With many a pointed blossom, rising, delicate, with the
perfume strong I love,

With every leaf a miracle…

—Walt Whitman

Just Breathe

Breath and life, and the opportunity to try. We cannot
take these things for granted. If you have nothing more,
you always have that.

—Alicia Keys

june

STAYING GROUNDED

Let the beauty we love be what we do. There are a
hundred ways to kneel and kiss the ground.

—RUMI

LISTENING TO STILLNESS

Know how to live within yourself: there is in your soul
a whole world of mysterious and enchanted thoughts;
they will be drowned by the noise without; daylight
will drive them away; listen to their singing and be
silent.

—FYODOR TYUTCHEV

WE HAVE IT ALL

3

I am the one whose praise echoes on high
I adorn all the earth
I am the breeze that nurtures all things green
I encourage blossoms to flourish with ripening fruits.
I am led by the spirit to feed the purest streams.
I am the rain coming from the dew
that causes the grasses to laugh with the joy of life. I call
forth tears, the aroma of holy work. I am the yearning
for good.

—Saint Hildegard of Bingen

First, let us reflect on our own work
and the effort of those who brought us this food.
Secondly, let us be aware of the quality of our deeds
as we receive this meal.
Thirdly, what is most essential
is the practice of mindfulness
which helps us transcend greed, anger, and delusion.
Fourthly, we appreciate this food
which sustains the good health of our body and mind.
Fifthly, in order to continue our practice for all beings
we accept this offering.

—ZEN BUDDHIST PRAYER

4

Stay Humble

You need only look at today's news to see how wild, unbridled success—coming when you're young and foolish, two things that often come together—can be a great detriment to a talented person. In my case, I appreciate being older when I became successful. It granted me a good deal of perspective by which to enjoy the success, but with humility.

—Morgan Freeman

Be Noisy!

Look, I really don't want to wax philosophic, but I will say that if you're alive, you got to flap your arms and legs, you got to jump around a lot, you got to make a lot of noise, because life is the very opposite of death. And therefore, as I see it, if you're quiet, you're not living. You've got to be noisy, or at least your thoughts should be noisy and colorful and lively.

—Mel Brooks

Done Greatly

7

Three keys to more abundant living: caring about others, daring for others, sharing with others.

—William A. Ward

In Your Hands

8

I thank you, O God, for your care and protection this day, keeping me from physical harm and spiritual corruption. I now place the work of the day into your hands, trusting that you will redeem my errors and turn my achievements to your glory. And I now ask you to work within me, trusting that you will use the hours of rest to create in me a new heart and new soul.

—Jacob Boehme

You Never Know

Live with awareness. Be open to all of life, even
when it's uncomfortable, unhappy, and imperfect.
Uncomfortable moments can motivate us to take action
that can result in meaningful experiences.

—Polly Campbell

A Rose Is a Rose Is a Rose

The roses under my window make no reference to
former roses or better ones; they are what they are; they
exist with God today. There is no time to them. There
is simply the rose; it is perfect in every moment of its
existence.

—Ralph Waldo Emerson

Rejoice in Abundance

Most worshipful God,
you created humans to walk the earth with its
abundance.
We beg of you, bless our family with riches and
prosperity.
May our farms yield an abundant harvest,
our animals and chickens multiply.
And you our forefathers, we invite you to look after our
well-being.
Ask and demand from us anything,
but protect us from all harm, illness, and evil spirits
which prowl the earth.
We will remember and honor you in the days to come.
We who partake of this abundant food rejoice
with those who rejoice and live long lives.
This is our heart's desire, and what our words express.
So let us feast.

—Prayer by the Kankana-ey Tribe
of the Igorot Indians

ACT ON THE GOOD

Gratitude promotes healing, harmony, peace, and joy.
It encourages forgiveness, patience, and goodwill. It is
a path that opens the opportunity for you to act on the
good in your life.

—MARY BETH SAMMONS

STAY OPEN TO THE UNEXPECTED

Should you shield the canyons from the windstorms,
you would never see the true beauty of their carvings.

—ELISABETH KÜBLER-ROSS

BE OF SERVICE

Service is the rent that you pay for room on this earth.

—SHIRLEY CHISHOLM

Now and Evermore

15

May the blessing of God rest upon you,
May his peace abide with you,
May his presence illuminate your heart,
Now and evermore.

—Sufi blessing

Good Company

16

Eating is not merely a material pleasure. Eating well
gives a spectacular joy to life and contributes immensely
to good will and happy companionship. It is of great
importance to the morale.

—Elsa Schiaparelli

Shining Through

It is naturally easy to be glad when life flows like a sweet song.

But great men are those who could smile when everything falls apart.

Since the test for the heart is to withstand problems which could come uninvited anytime. Thus the only smile worthy of a world honor is one that shines through the tears.

—Ella Wheeler Wilcox

A Winged Heart

Wake at dawn with a winged heart and give thanks for another day of loving.

—Kahlil Gibran

A World Filled with Blessings

No one can give
what he or she hasn't received.
So as we are blessed, we
bless the world
giving thanks for every living thing.

—HELEN SCHUCMAN

Togetherness

Thank you for the wind and rain
and for the pleasant weather,
thank you for this our food
and that we are together.

—MENNONITE BLESSING

The Needs of Others

Give us grateful hearts, our Father, for all thy mercies,
and make us mindful of the needs of others. Amen.

—FROM *THE BOOK OF COMMON PRAYER*

Bliss in Every Atom

It turns out that bliss—a second-by-second joy and gratitude at the gift of being alive, conscious—lies on the other side of crushing, crushing boredom. Pay close attention to the most tedious thing you can find (tax returns, televised golf), and, in waves, a boredom like you've never known will wash over you and just about kill you. Ride these out, and it's like stepping from black and white into color. Like water after days in the desert. Constant bliss in every atom.

—David Foster Wallace

Your Gratitude Hit List

Create a top ten list of the things you are most grateful for in your life. Carry it with you in your purse or pocket, or post it on your mirror, your refrigerator, or at your office to remind you daily of what you are grateful for.

—Brenda Knight

24

The winds of grace blow all the time. All we need to do is set our sails.

—SRI RAMAKRISHNA PARAMAHAMSA

MAY YOUR PRAYERS BE BEAUTIFUL

The garden is rich with diversity
With plants of a hundred families
In the space between the trees
With all the colors and fragrances
Basil, mint, and lavender,
God keep my remembrance pure,
Raspberry, Apple, Rose,
God fill my heart with love,
Dill, anise, tansy,
Holy winds blow in me.
Rhododendron, zinnia,
May my prayer be beautiful
May my remembrance O God
be an incense to thee
In the sacred grove of eternity
As I smell and remember
The ancient forest of earth.

—CHINOOK PSALTER

THE INFINITE YES

26

I thank you God for most this amazing
day: for the leaping greenly spirits of trees
and a blue true dream of sky; and for everything
which is natural which is infinite which is yes.

—E. E. CUMMINGS

REAPING WHAT YOU SOW

27

The first gathering of the garden in May of salads,
radishes and herbs made me feel like a mother about her
baby—how could anything so beautiful be mine?

—ALICE B. TOKLAS

IT WAS THE BEST OF DAYS

28

Reflect upon your present blessings, of which every man
has many; not on your past misfortunes, of which all
men have some.

—CHARLES DICKENS

Both Great and Small

Thankful may I ever be for benefits both great and
small—
And never fail in gratitude for that divinest gift of all:
The love of friends that I have known in times of failure
and success.
O may the first prayer of the day be always one of
thankfulness.

—Patience Strong

Words to Live By

As we express our gratitude, we must never forget that
the highest appreciation is not to utter words but to live
by them.

—John F. Kennedy

All's Right with the World

Summer is the time when one sheds one's tensions with one's clothes, and the right kind of day is jeweled balm for the battered spirit. A few of those days and you can become drunk with the belief that all's right with the world.

—Ada Louise Huxtable

What Sustains Us

Praised be my Lord for our Mother the Earth,
which sustains us and keeps us and brings forth diverse fruits,
And flowers of many colors—and grass.

—Saint Francis of Assisi

Thinking of Others

Reframe your thoughts on "giving." When we think of giving, we often think of donating money to a cause. But we can give numerous other gifts, such as our time, our presence, and our caring.

—Nina Lesowitz

Guided, Guarded, and Protected

May we live our lives beyond separation, knowing that nations and cultures are made up of individuals. May I be as one who rethinks my life, my actions, and aligns to the glory we are all capable of. May I follow where I am spiritually guided, and embrace what is new that is of love. May love flow through me and lend my individual life and light toward a better world.

—Jacqueline T. Snyder

Givers and Thanksgivers

Gratefulness brings joy to my life. How could I find joy in what I take for granted? So I stop taking for granted, and there is no end to the surprises I find. A grateful attitude is a creative one, because, in the final analysis, opportunity is the gift within the gift of every moment—the opportunity to see and hear and smell and touch and taste with pleasure.

There is no closer bond that the one that gratefulness celebrates, the bond between giver and thanksgiver. Everything is a gift. Grateful living is a celebration of the universal give-and-take of life, a limitless yes to belonging.

—Brother David Steindl-Rast

Play Well with Others

I think of life itself, now, as a wonderful play that I've written for myself, and so my purpose is to have the utmost fun playing my part.

—Shirley MacLaine

A GENEROUS HEART

We tire of those pleasures we take, but never of those we give.

—JOHN PETIT-SENN

THE MEANING OF LIFE

I had this thought that the only thing that God requires from us is to enjoy life and love. It doesn't matter if you accomplish anything. You don't have to do anything but appreciate that you're alive—and love. That's the whole point…you like to make music? Fine, go ahead. Make sure that if you do that, what people get from it is joy.

—PAUL SIMON

ALL I NEED IS A MIRACLE

A piece of the miracle process has been reserved for each of us.

—JIM ROHN

WILD ROSES IN EARLY JULY

I know there is poor and hideous suffering, and I've seen the hungry and the guns that go to war. I have lived pain, and my life can tell: I only deepen the wound of the world when I neglect to give thanks for early light dappled through leaves and the heavy perfume of wild roses in early July and the song of crickets on humid nights and the rivers that run and the stars that rise and the rain that falls and all the good things that a good God gives.

—ANN VOSKAMP

TAKE CHANCES

To be grateful means giving thanks for more than
just the things we want, but also for the things that
surmount our pride and stubbornness...

Sometimes just giving thanks for the mystery of it all
brings everything and everyone closer, the way suction
pulls streams of water together. So take a chance and
openly give thanks, even if you're not sure what for, and
feel the plenitude of all that is living brush up against
your heart.

—MARK NEPO

AWAKENINGS

Learn to turn to each person as the most sacred person
on Earth, and to each moment as the most sacred
moment that has ever been given to us. This moment
may never happen again, because no two moments are
ever alike. Are we perhaps awake a bit more, perhaps
breathing together with God?

—RESHAD FEILD

KEEP LOOKING

Stuff your eyes with wonder, live as if you'd drop dead
in ten seconds. See the world. It's more fantastic than
any dream made or paid for in factories.

—RAY BRADBURY

TIME ENOUGH

One day with life and heart
Is more than enough time to find a world.

—JAMES RUSSELL LOWELL

SET ASIDE YOUR CARES

But cease thy tears, bid ev'ry sigh depart,
And cast the load of anguish from thine heart:
From the cold shell of his great soul arise;
And look beyond, thou native of the skies…

—PHILLIS WHEATLEY

FOREVER GRATEFUL

I see the practice of gratitude as a way of keeping the heart open, but also a way of retaining our humanity in a growing world of neck-and-neck darkness and light, or evolutionary and de-evolutionary forces in a race here. But I'm forever grateful for the great gift of life itself, and also just seeing all the evolutionary possibilities that we have ahead of us.

—ANGELES ARRIEN

16

FOR EVERYTHING, THERE IS A SEASON

Live in each season as it passes; breathe the air, drink the drink, taste the fruit, and resign yourself to the influences of each.

—HENRY DAVID THOREAU

The Source of All Life

Whenever the Confederate Lords shall assemble for the purpose of holding a council, the Onondaga Lords shall open it by expressing their gratitude to their cousin Lords and greeting them, and they shall make an address and offer thanks to the earth where men dwell, to the streams of water, the pools, the springs and the lakes, to the maize and the fruits, to the medicinal herbs and trees, to the forest trees for their usefulness, to the animals that serve as food and give their pelts for clothing, to the great winds and the lesser winds, to the Thunderers, to the Sun, the mighty warrior, to the moon, to the messengers of the Creator who reveal his wishes and to the Great Creator who dwells in the heavens above, who gives all the things useful to men, and who is the source and the ruler of health and life. Then shall the Onondaga Lords declare the council open. The council shall not sit after darkness has set in.

—From the Iroquois Confederacy Constitution

LEAN IN

Earth, when I am about to die
I lean upon you.
Earth, while I am alive
I depend upon you.

—ASHANTI PRAYER

A LIST OF LOVE

Stop for a moment and be thankful for the giver behind
the gift. Make a list of the people in your life who made
you happy today.

—BRENDA KNIGHT

Last Watch of the Night

A great star has fallen into my lap...
We want to wake through the night,

To pray in languages
Notched like harps.

We want to be reconciled with the night—
God overflows so much.

Our hearts are children,
They may rest tiredsweet.

And our lips want to kiss,
Why do you hesitate?

Do not join my heart to yours—
Always your blood reddens my cheeks.

We want to be reconciled with the night,
When we embrace, we do not die.

A great star has fallen into my lap.

—Else Lasker-Schüler

With a Full Heart

Gratitude is the memory of the heart.

—Jean Baptiste Massieu

The Whole of Creation

Join the whole creation of animate things in a deep, heartfelt joy that you are alive, that you see the sun, that you are in this glorious earth which nature has made so beautiful, and which is yours to conquer and enjoy.

—Sir William Osler

Jars of Honey

Piglet noticed that even though he had a Very Small Heart, it could hold a rather large amount of Gratitude.

—A. A. Milne

LOOK FORWARD TO UNEXPECTED SURPRISES

25 I find that the more willing I am to be grateful for the small things in life, the bigger stuff just seems to show up from unexpected sources, and I am constantly looking forward to each day with all the surprises that keep coming my way!

—Louise L. Hay

MAY YOU ALWAYS BE BLESSED

26 For food in a world where many walk in hunger
For faith in a world where many walk in fear
For friends in a world where many walk alone
We give you humble thanks, oh Lord.

—World Hunger grace

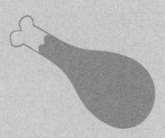

Big Sky Mind

I hope it is true that a man can die and yet not only live in others but give them life, and not only life, but that great consciousness of life.

—Jack Kerouac

Time Does Tell

A few years' experience will convince us that those things which at the time they happened we regarded as our greatest misfortunes have proved our greatest blessings.

—George Mason

THE QUIET, UNSPOKEN DEPTHS

29

For the longest time, I thought gratitude was something
that had to be extended to another for it to be legitimate.
Just like the literal act of hanging a flower basket on a
door knob. The power of gratitude has grown in my life.
I appreciate its boldness in the quiet, unspoken depths
and its ability to buoy another by being articulated.

—MARY ANNE RADMACHER

30

ACTS OF BEAUTY

Saying "thank you" creates love.

—DAPHNE ROSE KINGMA

FINDING THE GOOD IN EVERYTHING

And this our life, exempt from public haunt
Finds tongues in trees, books in running brooks,
Sermons in stones and good in every thing.

31

—WILLIAM SHAKESPEARE

august

ALL THAT WE ARE

This being human is a guest house.
Every morning a new arrival.

A joy, a depression, a meanness,
some momentary awareness comes
as an unexpected visitor.

Welcome and entertain them all!
Even if they're a crowd of sorrows,
who violently sweep your house
empty of its furniture,
still, treat each guest honorably.
He may be clearing you out
for some new delight.

The dark thought, the shame, the malice,
meet them at the door laughing,
and invite them in.

Be grateful for whoever comes,
because each has been sent
as a guide from beyond.

—RUMI

COUNT YOURSELF LUCKY

When life's problems seem overwhelming, look around and see what other people are coping with. You may consider yourself fortunate.

—ANN LANDERS

THANKFULNESS DEFINED

Gratitude (noun): The quality of being thankful; readiness to show appreciation for and to return kindness; gratefulness, thankfulness, thanks, appreciation, indebtedness; recognition, acknowledgement, credit.

—MARY ANNE RADMACHER

God Adores His Creations

4

I think God might be a little prejudiced.
For once he asked me to join Him on a walk
through this world,
and we gazed into every heart on this earth,
and I noticed He lingered a bit longer
before any face that was weeping,
and before any eyes that were laughing.
And sometimes when we passed
a soul in worship
God too would kneel down.
I have come to learn:
God adores his creation.

—Saint Francis of Assisi

The Art of Happiness

5

The art of being happy lies in the power of extracting
happiness from common things.

—Henry Ward Beecher

Kabbalah in Hebrew means "to accept." Kabbalah teaches us how to flow with God's work by accepting it. The oyster holds the same secret; it teaches us to accept our weaknesses and disabilities. We are perfect in our imperfections; that is the secret paradox of life. What makes us perfect is the ability to grow, and we can only grow if we are not yet perfect. As long as we have some imperfections, we are participating in God's creation.

That is the key of life and that is the Jewel in the Lotus. We often spend too much time in gratitude for what is going well in our life, but as God is One, the perfect and imperfect in you are also one. Spend some time focusing on showing your gratitude toward the imperfections that make you so perfect.

—GAHL SASSON

GIVE GIVE GIVE

7

Life engenders life. Energy creates energy. It is by
spending oneself that one becomes rich.

—SARAH BERNHARDT

FREEDOM

8

Are you jealous of the ocean's generosity?
Why would you refuse to give this
joy to anyone?

Fish don't hold the sacred liquid in cups!
They swim the huge fluid freedom.

—RUMI

Stop, Look, and Listen

Listen
with the night falling we are saying thank you
we are stopping on the bridges to bow from the railings
we are running out of the glass rooms
with our mouths full of food to look at the sky
and say thank you...

—W. S. Merwin

Simplicity

That which creates a happy life
Is substance left, not gained by strife...

—Mildmay Fane

In Everything Is Its Opposite

When starting out, don't worry about not having enough
money. Limited funds are a blessing, not a curse. Nothing
encourages creative thinking in quite the same way.

—H. Jackson Brown

GRAINS OF ABUNDANCE

Blessed art thou O Lord my God, King of the universe,
who brings forth the bread from the earth.

—JEWISH PRAYER

BEING TRULY ALIVE

We can only be said to be alive in those moments when
our hearts are conscious of our treasures.

—THORNTON WILDER

THE PRIME VIRTUE

The essence of all beautiful art, all great art, is gratitude.

—FRIEDRICH NIETZSCHE

THE THREE TREASURES

First, seventy-two labors brought us this food;
we should know how it comes to us.
Second, as we receive this offering,
we should consider whether our virtue and practice
deserve it. Third, as we desire the natural order of mind
to be free from clinging, we must be free from greed.
Fourth, to support our life, we take this food.
Fifth, to attain our way, we take this food.

First, this food is for the Three Treasures.
Second, it is for our teachers, parents, nation,
and all sentient beings.
Third, it is for all beings in the six worlds.
Thus, we eat this food with everyone.
We eat to stop all evil, to practice good,
to save all sentient beings,
and to accomplish our Buddha Way.

—Buddhist prayer

Equal and Opposite

There is a Law of Gratitude, and it is…the natural principle that action and reaction are always equal and in opposite directions. The grateful outreaching of your mind in thankful praise to supreme intelligence is a liberation or expenditure of force. It cannot fail to reach that to which it is addressed, and the reaction is an instantaneous movement toward you.

—Wallace Delois Wattles

The Great Work

Leader: Do what thou wilt shall be the whole of the Law.
All: What is thy will?
Leader: It is my will to eat and to drink.
All: To what end?
Leader: That I may fortify my body thereby.
All: To what end?
Leader: That I may accomplish the Great Work.
All: Love is the law, love under will.

—From *The Book of the Law*

THERE ARE MANY KINDS OF RICHES

I thank fate for having made me born poor. Poverty taught me the true value of the gifts useful to life.

—ANATOLE FRANCE

IT'S ALL GOOD

Saying thank you is more than good manners. It is good spirituality.

—ALFRED PAINTER

CHANGE FOR THE BETTER

If you can change the way people think. The way they see themselves. The way they see the world. If you do that, you can change the way people live their lives. That's the only lasting thing you can create.

—CHUCK PALAHNIUK

POETRY IN MOTION

21 The world is full of poetry.
The air is living with its spirit,
And the waves dance to the music of its melodies,
And sparkle in its brightness.

—JAMES GATES PERCIVAL

HIDDEN BEAUTY

22 When your inner eyes open, you can find immense
beauty hidden within the inconsequential details of
daily life. When your inner ears open, you can hear the
subtle, lovely music of the universe everywhere you go.

—TIMOTHY RAY MILLER

LIFE IS THANKFULNESS

The lands around my dwelling
Are more beautiful
From the day
When it is given me to see
Faces I have never seen before.
All is more beautiful,
All is more beautiful,
And life is thankfulness.
These guests of mine
Make my house grand.

—ESKIMO PRAYER

SATISFACTION GUARANTEED

It is wealth to be content.

—LAO TZU

What Good Can I Do Today?

25

I expect to pass through life but once. If therefore, there be any kindness I can show, or any good thing I can do to any fellow being, let me do it now, and not defer or neglect it, as I shall not pass this way again.

—William Penn

The Art of Surrender

26

If you let yourself be absorbed completely, if you surrender completely to the moments as they pass, you live more richly those moments.

—Anne Morrow Lindbergh

A Chorus of Gratitude

27

When a man is singing and cannot lift his voice, and another comes and sings with him, another who can lift his voice, the first will be able to lift his voice too. That is the secret of the bond between spirits.

—Hasidic saying

WEEDS AND WONDER

May your life be like a wildflower, growing freely in the beauty and joy of each day.

—NATIVE AMERICAN PROVERB

LEARNING AS WE GO

Our real blessings often appear to us in the shape of pains, losses and disappointments; but let us have patience and we soon shall see them in their proper figures.

—JOSEPH ADDISON

THANK GODDESS!

30

All life is your own,
All fruits of the earth
Are fruits of your womb,
Your union, your dance.
Lady and Lord,
We thank you for blessings and abundance.
Join with us, Feast with us, Enjoy with us!
Blessed be.

—STARHAWK

THANK GOD FOR WHAT YOU HAVE

I'm not the holiest person you've ever met, but I thank
God for what I've had and what I've got. I'm grateful for
it all—the windows, the light, the street, and the cars. I
know I've been looked after in this life.

—B. B. KING

31

september

BE CREATIVE

For thirty consecutive days make a list of at least five things you are grateful for. Include on each list one item you have never before expressed gratitude for (dental floss, your toenails), as well as one item that is a gift, which was hidden in a challenge, problem, or disappointment (the gift of a traffic jam may be patience, the gift of a disagreement may be learning to accept another point of view, etc.). Be creative.

—POLLY CAMPBELL

BLESSING IN EVERY HEART

The unthankful heart...discovers no mercies; but let the thankful heart sweep through the day and, as the magnet finds the iron, so it will find, in every hour, some heavenly blessings!

—HENRY WARD BEECHER

GOOD AND JOYFUL THINGS

Bless these Thy gifts, most gracious God,
from whom all goodness springs;
Make clean our hearts and feed our souls
with good and joyful things.

—TRADITIONAL CHRISTIAN GRACE

SO MUCH TO BE GRATEFUL FOR

When something disappointing happened, my mother
would remind me not to let that become my focus.
There's still so much to be grateful for.

—KATHERINE HEIGL

5

Look at nature. Nature is filled with wheat fields. Nature is filled with fruit trees. Nature is filled with all its gifts. It is abundant in every way. You are a willing receiver of these fruits, of these gifts. In return, is it too much to ask for you to give your blessings to the Earth Mother? She needs them. She needs them right now. Dance on her. Drum on her. Love on her. She needs you. She needs your love, your respect, your trust. She needs you to enjoy her. Give her lots of love, for she has been ignored to the nth degree. Your buildings—not one of them is as beautiful as one of her mountains. See with your eyes the beauty she has given to you; that she gives to you every single day. Give her love and attention and she will give it back to you in countless ways, in ways that you can barely imagine...

—TONY BURROUGHS

LET FAITH BE YOUR BRIDGE

6

Let gratitude be the pillow upon which you kneel to say your nightly prayer. And let faith be the bridge you build to overcome evil and welcome good.

—MAYA ANGELOU

SHOWING APPRECIATION

7

Make it a habit to tell people thank you. To express your appreciation, sincerely and without the expectation of anything in return. Truly appreciate those around you, and you'll soon find many others around you. Truly appreciate life, and you'll find that you have more of it.

—RALPH MARSTON

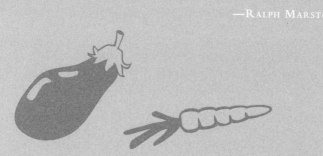

TEND YOUR OWN GARDEN

All is miracle. The stupendous order of nature, the revolution of a hundred millions of worlds around a million of suns, the activity of light, the life of animals, all are grand and perpetual miracles.

—VOLTAIRE

DOUBLE HAPPINESS

I would maintain that thanks are the highest form of thought, and that gratitude is happiness doubled by wonder.

—G. K. CHESTERTON

And so I Climb

Because when death sits on your shoulder each day,
whispering, urging you to your end, there is no time
to lose, so much light to grasp for, strive for, struggle
to embrace. We are struggling with light. And yet we
are only human after all, so terribly flawed and foolish,
selfish and ridiculous. Sobriety can be so messy. At times,
I have seemed to myself the most awful of persons.
But even then I am ascending, even then I am going
up a ladder of light with eyes wide open and hands
outstretched, to clasp the next rung up. And I climb.

—Alan Kaufman

God in a Word

Like golden mist, the west lights up
The window. The diligent manuscript
Awaits, already laden with infinity.
Someone is building God in the twilight.

—Jorge Luis Borges

BOLD NEW WORLDS

Each friend represents a world in us, a world possibly not born until they arrive, and it is only by this meeting that a new world is born.

—ANAÏS NIN

ASPIRATION AND INSPIRATION

Grace, growth, and gratitude: these are my highest aspirations.

—GLORIA ARLISS

YOUR HEART'S DESIRE

Every moment of your life is infinitely creative and the universe is endlessly bountiful. Just put forth a clear enough request, and everything your heart truly desires must come to you.

—SHAKTI GAWAIN

Love's Labors

Be glad of life because it gives you the chance to love
and to work and to play and to look at the stars.

—Henry Van Dyke

On Earth as It Is in Heaven

God has two dwellings; one in heaven, and the other in
a meek and thankful heart.

—Isaak Walton

It Is Written

Miracles are a retelling in small letters of the very same
story which is written across the whole world in letters
too large for some of us to see.

—C. S. Lewis

15

16

17

Each Bud and Blossom

18

Farewell, green fields and happy groves,
Where flocks have took delight.
Where lambs have nibbled, silent moves
The feet of angels bright;
Unseen they pour blessing
And joy without ceasing,
On each bud and blossom,
And each sleeping bosom.

—WILLIAM BLAKE

Happiness Is an Inside Job

Happiness depends, as Nature shows,
Less on exterior things than most suppose.

—WILLIAM COWPER

How to Be Truly Alive

A man without ambition is dead. A man with ambition but no love is dead. A man with ambition and love for his blessings here on earth is ever so alive.

—Pearl Bailey

20

Keeping Track of Time

The only way to live is to accept each minute as an unrepeatable miracle, which is exactly what it is: a miracle and unrepeatable.

—Storm Jameson

21

West with the Night

22

And the night of darkness
And the dawn of light,
Meeting, joining one another,
Helpmates ever, they.
All is beautiful,
All is beautiful,
All is beautiful, indeed.

—from "The Navajo Song of the Earth"

Live Your Way to the Answers

23

Have patience with everything unresolved in your heart
and to try to love the questions themselves as if they
were locked rooms or books written in a very foreign
language. Don't search for the answers, which could not
be given to you now, because you would not be able to
live them. And the point is, to live everything. Live the
questions now. Perhaps then, someday far in the future,
you will gradually, without even noticing it, live your
way into the answer.

—Rainer Maria Rilke

THE SOUL'S TRUE WORTH

You have not lived a perfect day, even though you have earned your money, unless you have done something for someone who will never be able to repay you.

—RUTH SMELTZER

FIELDS OF BARLEY

For the Lord your God is bringing you into a good land, a land of flowing streams, with springs and underground waters welling up in valleys and hills, a land of wheat and barley, of vines and fig trees and pomegranates, a land of olive trees and honey, a land where you may eat bread without scarcity, where you will lack nothing, a land whose stones are iron and from whose hills you may mine copper. You shall eat your fill and bless the Lord your God for the good land he has given you.

—DEUTERONOMY 8:7–10

Blossom Where You Are

26

Every flower about a house certifies to the refinement of somebody. Every vine climbing and blossoming tells of love and joy.

—Robert Ingersoll

Catch Them If You Can

During difficult transitions, our natural tendency is often to contract and grow rigid. In this state we seem to only be able to focus on the negatives. We think about the despair and torment of the death of a loved one, but not the wonderful moments spent together. We think of the heartbreak of a relationship ending, but not of the exhilaration and freedom of being unattached. We might even scold our loved ones, or our friends, or coworkers for something minor or insignificant when we wallow in such negativity. But it is in these moments specifically that gratitude can be used to alter this way of thinking. Finding positives and accentuating them is the easiest way to turn those proverbial frowns upside down and gray skies back to blue. Try catching someone doing

27

something right for a change, not something wrong. Giving praise for a job well done lifts all parties involved and is the easiest way to say, "Thank You," without actually having to say it.

—BRENDA KNIGHT

PHILOSOPHY 101

Gratitude is not only the greatest of virtues, but the parent of all the others.

—CICERO

GIVING YOURSELF PERMISSION

I've permitted myself to learn and to fail with some regularity. And that is probably the one thing I was given, and that I'm still grateful for.

—JOHN MALKOVICH

30

When we eat the good bread,
we are eating months of sunlight,
weeks of rain and snow from the sky,
richness out of the earth.
We should be great, each of us radiant,
full of music and full of stories.
Able to run the way clouds do, able to
dance like the snow and the rain.
But nobody takes time to think that he eats all
these things and that sun, rain,
snow are all a part of himself.

—Monica Shannon

october

GOOD MANNERS

If the only prayer you say in your whole life is "Thank you," that would suffice.

—MEISTER ECKHART

THE GREAT RIVER

Lord, we brought in the harvest.

The rain watered the earth, the sun drew cassava and corn out of the clay. Your mercy showered blessing after blessing over our country. Creeks grew into rivers; swamps became lakes. Healthy fat cows graze on the green sea of the savanna. The rain smoothed out the clay walls, the mosquitoes drowned in the high waters.

Lord, the yam is fat like meat, the cassava melts on the tongue, oranges burst in their peels, dazzling and bright.

Lord, nature gives thanks, Your creatures give thanks.

Your praise rises in us like the great river.

—WEST AFRICAN PRAYER

JUST BE

Try a walking meditation the next chance you get.
Whether it is a walk around the block, in a park, or on
the beach, just begin walking and empty your mind of
tasks, troubles, and worries and *just be*. Observe your
surroundings with fresh eyes and enjoy the beauty
around you, even if it is a flower blooming through a
crack in the sidewalk.

—NINA LESOWITZ

3

FAITHFULLY

I am thankful before You,
Living and Sustaining Ruler,
Who returned my soul to me with mercy.
Your faithfulness is great.

—*MODEH ANI*, A JEWISH MORNING PRAYER

4

WALKING ON SUNSHINE

5 Do not anticipate trouble, or worry about what may
never happen. Keep in the sunlight.

—BENJAMIN FRANKLIN

NATURE'S WAY

6 Expressing gratitude is a natural state of being and
reminds us that we are all connected.

—VALERIE ELSTER

GOOD MEDICINE

7 Gratitude is a vaccine, an antitoxin, and an antiseptic.

—JOHN HENRY JOWETT

CLIMB THE MOUNTAINS

Climb the mountains and get their good tidings:
Nature's peace will flow into you as sunshine into
flowers, the winds will blow their freshness into you,
and the storms, their energy and cares will drop off like
autumn leaves.

—JOHN MUIR

WITH A LITTLE HELP FROM OUR FRIENDS

I feel really grateful to the people who encouraged
me and helped me develop. Nobody can succeed on
their own.

—SHERYL SANDBERG

GOOD HARVESTS

Heap high the farmer's wintry hoard!
Heap high the golden corn!
No richer gift has Autumn poured
From out her lavish horn!...

But let the good old crop adorn
The hills our fathers trod;
Still let us, for His golden corn,
Send up our thanks to God!

—JOHN GREENLEAF WHITTIER

EVERYWHERE YOU LOOK

There is not a flower that opens, not a seed that falls
into the ground, and not an ear of wheat that nods on
the end of its stalk in the wind that does not preach and
proclaim the greatness and the mercy of God to the
whole world.

—THOMAS MERTON

BALMS TO THE HEART

It is more blessed to give than to receive.

—ACTS 20:35

SONGS OF GRATITUDE

I always say that writing, for me, is like going to church. When I'm out of my own way, when my ego is hushed, when my propensity for judging myself and editing myself is silenced for a moment, I'm feeling pretty close to God and everything's good. To find a lyric that comes together to teach me about myself is a real blessing. I wrote a lot of my last record (*Detours*) at six in the morning, right after feeding my baby, really enjoying the quiet and appreciating the thoughts that come at that hour.

—SHERYL CROW

BREAKING BREAD WITH FRIENDS

14

A circle of friends is a blessed thing.
Sweet is the breaking of bread with friends.
For the honor of their presence at our board
We are deeply grateful, Lord.

Thanks be to Thee for friendship shared,
Thanks be to Thee for food prepared.
Bless Thou the cup, bless Thou the bread;
Thy blessing rest upon each head.

—WALTER RAUSCHENBUSCH

COURTESIES, GREAT AND SMALL

15

Courtesies of a small and trivial character are the ones
which strike deepest in the grateful and appreciating
heart.

—HENRY CLAY

WITH GRACE

Each day offers us the gift of being a special occasion if we can simply learn that as well as giving, it is blessed to receive with grace and a grateful heart.

—SARAH BAN BREATHNACH

16

GIVE THEE THANKS

O thou cereal deity, we worship thee.
Thou hast grown very well this year,
and thy flavor will be sweet.
Thou art good.
The goddess of fire will be glad, and
we also shall rejoice greatly.

—AINU PRAYER

17

THE WHOLE WORLD BELONGS TO YOU

When you realize there is nothing lacking, the whole world belongs to you.

—LAO TZU

18

THE MORE THEY GIVE, THE MORE THEY POSSESS

19

This is the miracle that happens every time to those who really love: the more they give, the more they possess.

—RAINER MARIA RILKE

ENLIGHTENMENT FOR ALL

20

No individual exists in their own nature, independent of all other factors of life. Each has the totality of the Universe at their base. All individuals have, therefore, the whole Universe as their common ground, and this universality becomes conscious in the experience of enlightenment, in which the individual awakens into their own true all-embracing nature.

—LAMA GOVINDA

Love Is All Around

Love is easy. You can't resist love. You get an idea, someone says something, and you're in love. I went to dinner in Denver about twenty years ago and heard the lady at the next table say to her friends, "Oh, my God, I'll bet dogs think every day is Christmas." I went up to her and said, "Madam, thank you. You've just given me a title. I'm going back to my hotel, and I'm going to write a book called *Dogs Think That Every Day Is Christmas*." That's how these things happen.

—Ray Bradbury

21

Into the Mystic

Nature: the Unseen Intelligence which loved us into being, and is disposing of us by the same token.

—Elbert Hubbard

22

STEWARDS OF THE EARTH

23

We give thanks for the Sun even when
behind clouds it hides.
We give thanks for the Wind
though it bends the birches low.
We give thanks for Rain gentle or torrential.
We give thanks for the Earth.
For its Beauty and Glory and Power we give thanks.
Give us grace to be good stewards of this
our Inheritance.

—ANNABELLE WOODARD

TAKING TIME

24

Even if something is left undone, everyone must take
time to sit still and watch the leaves turn.

—ELIZABETH LAWRENCE

THANK YOU AND GOOD NIGHT

Go to bed with gratitude. Think about all you
appreciate from the day that just passed, breathing
deeply and relaxing as you do so.

—MARY BETH SAMMONS

25

SIMPLE PLEASURES

And forget not that the earth delights to feel your bare
feet and the winds long to play with your hair.

—KAHLIL GIBRAN

26

365 DAYS OF THANK YOU

For each new morning with its light,
For rest and shelter of the night,
For health and food, for love and friends,
For everything Thy goodness sends.

—RALPH WALDO EMERSON

27

GIVING AND LIVING

28

I absolutely believe in the power of tithing and giving back. My own experience about all the blessings I've had in my life is that the more I give away, the more that comes back. That is the way life works, and that is the way energy works.

—KEN BLANCHARD

A PEACEFUL HEART

Geese appear high over us,
pass, and the sky closes. Abandon,
as in love or sleep, holds
them to their way, clear
in the ancient faith: what we need
is here. And we pray, not
for new earth or heaven, but to be
quiet in heart, and in eye,
clear. What we need is here.

29

—WENDELL BERRY

ACCENT ON THE POSITIVE

Over and over, I marvel at the blessings of my life: each year has grown better than the last.

—LAWRENCE WELK

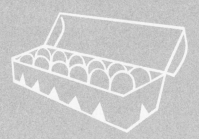

BANKING ON BLESSINGS

I am grateful for what I am and have. My thanksgiving is perpetual…O how I laugh when I think of my vague indefinite riches. No run on my bank can drain it, for my wealth is not possession but enjoyment.

—HENRY DAVID THOREAU

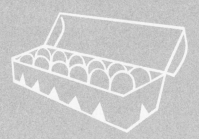

november

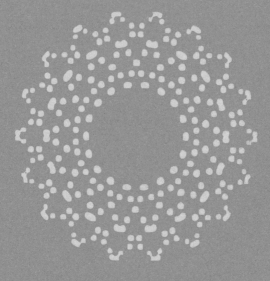

Remember to Have Fun

I wake up every day with a sense of gratitude and a sense of newness. Every day is a new day for me. I don't really spend time anticipating, and I'm not victimized by memories, so it's fun to be alive. You should try it.

—Deepak Chopra

Legacies

The highest tribute to the dead is not grief but gratitude.

—Thornton Wilder

Never Delay Happiness!

Try to be happy in this present moment, and put not off being so to a time to come—as though that time should be of another make from this which has already come and is ours.

—Thomas Fuller

THE TRUTH ABOUT LIFE

Oh God
Help me
to believe
the truth about myself
no matter
how beautiful it is!

—MACRINA WIEDERKEHR

4

LIVING IN LOVE

Love talking. Love listening. Love eating. Love feeding.
Love storing up. Love giving away. Love hugs, direct
gazes, soft seats, giggles and belly laughs. Love nature
and dreams. Love the real and the imaginary and the
blurred lines between the two. Love the possibilities for
herself and others.

—ALICE WALKER

LIMITLESS JOY

6

Love the moment, and the energy of that moment will spread beyond all boundaries.

—SISTER CORITA KENT

BLESSINGS PILED HIGH

7

The Blessing of God
rest upon all those who have been kind to us,
have cared for us, have worked for us, have served us,
and have shared our bread with us at this table.
Our merciful God,
reward all of them in your own way.
For yours is the glory and honor forever.
Amen.

—SAINT CYRIL

Truth and Fiction

Both in good fiction and in life, you may not always get what you want, but you will probably get what you need. We should be grateful for these things.

—Neil Gaiman

De Profundis

All the things of the universe are perfect miracles, each as profound as any.

—Walt Whitman

Look Out Your Window

One of the most tragic things I know about human nature is that all of us tend to put off living. We are all dreaming of some magical rose garden over the horizon—instead of enjoying the roses blooming outside our windows today.

—Dale Carnegie

Worrying Isn't Worth It

Difficult times have helped me to understand better than before, how infinitely rich and beautiful life is in every way, and that so many things that one goes worrying about are of no importance whatsoever.

—ISAK DINESEN

Be at Peace with Yourself

Everything is a miracle. It is a miracle that one does not dissolve in one's bath like a lump of sugar.

—JOSEPH GORDON-LEVITT

Take Nothing for Granted

When my parents were liberated, four years before I was born, they found that the ordinary world outside the camp had been eradicated. There was no more simple meal, no thing was less than extraordinary: a fork, a mattress, a clean shirt, a book. Not to mention such things that can make one weep: an orange, meat and vegetables, hot water. There was no ordinariness to return to, no refuge from the blinding potency of things, an apple screaming its sweet juice.

—Anne Michaels

The Comforts of Grace

God who invites us always to spiritual delights,
give blessing over your gifts so that we might deserve
to partake in the blessed things which ought to be
added to your name.

Let your gifts refresh us, Lord,
and let your grace comfort us.

—Early Christian grace

KEEPING IT REAL

I love what many traditional peoples have said: that there are really three medicines that you should put in your medicine bundle every day, which are the power of genuine acknowledgment and gratitude, genuine apology, and the spirit of laughter and joy. And cross-culturally, there's not a culture in the world that doesn't have a means of saying thank you.

—ANGELES ARRIEN

PURE GENIUS

Everything is a miracle. It is a miracle that one does not dissolve in one's bath like a lump of sugar.

—PABLO PICASSO

HARVEST HOME

For the hay and the corn
and the wheat that is reaped,
For the labor well done,
and the barns that are heaped,
For the sun and the dew
and the sweet honeycomb,
For the rose and the song,
and the harvest brought home—
Thanksgiving! Thanksgiving!

—Traditional English hymn

GLORY IN YOUR NAME

18

Almighty and gracious Father,
we give you thanks
for the fruits of the earth in their season
and for the labors of those who harvest them.
Make us, we pray,
faithful stewards of your great bounty,
for the provision of our necessities
and the relief of all who are in need,
to the glory of your Name;
through Jesus Christ our Lord,
who lives and reigns with
you and the Holy Spirit,
one God, now and for ever. Amen.

—FROM *THE BOOK OF COMMON PRAYER*

SIMPLE ABUNDANCE

19

Where there is great love, there are always miracles.

—WILLA CATHER

A Renewable Resource

Gratitude to gratitude always gives birth.

—Sophocles

Let Us Give Thanks

Eternal Spirit of Justice and Love,
At this time of Thanksgiving we would be aware
of our dependence on the earth and on the
sustaining presence of other human beings
both living and gone before us.
As we partake of bread and wine, may we
remember that there are many for whom
sufficient bread is a luxury, or for whom
wine, when attainable, is only an escape.
Let our thanksgiving for Life's bounty include a
commitment to changing the world, that
those who are now hungry may be filled and
those without hope may be given courage.
Amen.

—Prayer by the Congregation of Abraxas

22

Let this day, from this time forth, as long as our Banner of Stars floats on the breeze, be the grand THANKSGIVING HOLIDAY of our nation, when the noise and tumult of worldliness may be exchanged for the laugh of happy children, the glad greetings of family reunion, and the humble gratitude of the Christian heart…let us consecrate the day to benevolence of action, by sending good gifts to the poor, and doing those deeds of charity that will, for one day, make every American home the place of plenty and rejoicing. These seasons of refreshing are of inestimable advantage to the popular heart; and, if rightly managed, will greatly aid and strengthen public harmony of feeling. Let the people of all the States and Territories sit down together to the "feast of fat things," and drink, in the sweet draught of joy and gratitude to the Divine giver of all our blessings, the pledge of renewed love to the Union, and to each other; and of peace and goodwill to all men.

—SARAH JOSEPHA HALE,
THE "MOTHER OF AMERICAN THANKSGIVING"

GROW YOUR OWN GRATITUDE

Our rural ancestors, with little blest,
Patient of labor when the end was rest,
Indulged the day that housed their annual grain,
With feasts, and off'rings, and a thankful strain.

—ALEXANDER POPE

THESE GREAT THINGS

The year that is drawing towards its close, has been
filled with the blessings of fruitful fields and healthful
skies. To these bounties, which are so constantly
enjoyed that we are prone to forget the source from
which they come, others have been added, which are
of so extraordinary a nature, that they cannot fail to
penetrate and soften even the heart which is habitually
insensible to the ever watchful providence of Almighty
God. In the midst of a civil war of unequaled magnitude
and severity, which has sometimes seemed to foreign
States to invite and to provoke their aggression, peace
has been preserved with all nations, order has been
maintained, the laws have been respected and obeyed,

23

24

and harmony has prevailed everywhere except in the theatre of military conflict; while that theatre has been greatly contracted by the advancing armies and navies of the Union. Needful diversions of wealth and of strength from the fields of peaceful industry to the national defence, have not arrested the plough, the shuttle or the ship; the axe has enlarged the borders of our settlements, and the mines, as well of iron and coal as of the precious metals, have yielded even more abundantly than heretofore. Population has steadily increased, notwithstanding the waste that has been made in the camp, the siege and the battle-field; and the country, rejoicing in the consiousness of augmented strength and vigor, is permitted to expect continuance of years with large increase of freedom. No human counsel hath devised nor hath any mortal hand worked out these great things. They are the gracious gifts of the Most High God, who, while dealing with us in anger for our sins, hath nevertheless remembered mercy. It has seemed to me fit and proper that they should be solemnly, reverently and gratefully acknowledged as with one heart and one voice by the whole American People. I do therefore invite my fellow citizens in every part of the

United States, and also those who are at sea and those who are sojourning in foreign lands, to set apart and observe the last Thursday of November next, as a day of Thanksgiving and Praise to our beneficent Father who dwelleth in the Heavens. And I recommend to them that while offering up the ascriptions justly due to Him for such singular deliverances and blessings, they do also, with humble penitence for our national perverseness and disobedience, commend to His tender care all those who have become widows, orphans, mourners or sufferers in the lamentable civil strife in which we are unavoidably engaged, and fervently implore the interposition of the Almighty Hand to heal the wounds of the nation and to restore it as soon as may be consistent with the Divine purposes to the full enjoyment of peace, harmony, tranquility and Union.

—ABRAHAM LINCOLN

JOY AND LAUGHTER

25 Gratitude helps you to grow and expand; gratitude brings joy and laughter into your life and into the lives of all those around you.

—EILEEN CADDY

THE TASTE OF HAPPINESS

26 All we can touch, swallow, or say
aids in our crossing to God
and helps unveil the soul.

—SAINT TERESA OF AVILA

Surprised by Joy

I admit to being, at times,
Suddenly, and without the slightest warning,
Exceedingly happy.

—Charles Simic

Savor It All

Exhaust the little moment. Soon it dies.
And be it gash or gold it will not come
Again in this identical disguise.

—Gwendolyn Brooks

The Sweet Life

29

O you that still have rain and sun,
Kisses of children and of wife,
And the good earth to tread upon,
And the mere sweetness of life,
Forget not us, who gave all these
For something dearer, and for you.

—Laurence Binyon

Be of Good Cheer

30

In our daily lives, we must see that it is not happiness
that makes us grateful, but the gratefulness that makes
us happy.

—Albert Clarke

december

To Love That Well

That time of year thou mayst in me behold
When yellow leaves, or none or few, do hang
Upon those boughs which shake against the cold,
Bare ruined choirs, where late the sweet birds sang.
In me thou see'st the twilight of such day
As after sunset fadeth in the west;
Which by and by black night doth take away,
Death's second self, that seals up all in rest.
In me thou see'st the glowing of such fire,
That on the ashes of his youth doth lie,
As the deathbed whereon it must expire,
Consumed with that which it was nourished by.
This thou perceiv'st, which makes thy love more strong,
To love that well which thou must leave ere long.

—William Shakespeare

GIFTS OF THE HEART

Kindness is a hard thing to give away; it keeps coming
back to the giver.

—RALPH SCOTT

MAKING A LIFE

From what we get, we can make a living; what we give,
however, makes a life.

—ARTHUR ASHE

ENOUGH FOR ALL

Blessed are you, Lord.
You have fed us from our earliest days;
you give food to every living creature.
Fill our hearts with joy and delight.

—EARLY CHRISTIAN PRAYER

2

3

4

A SERENITY PRAYER

I cannot lose anything in this place of abundance I found.

—SAINT CATHERINE OF SIENA

PARADISIO

The more love that it finds, the more it gives itself; so that, as we grow clear and open, the more complete the joy of heaven is.

—DANTE

LIVING FOR TODAY

Yesterday is ashes; tomorrow wood. Only today does the fire burn brightly.

—ESKIMO SAYING

ROADS NOT TAKEN

I do not ask to walk smooth paths
nor bear an easy load.
I pray for strength and fortitude
to climb the rock-strewn road.

Give me such courage and I can scale
the headiest peaks alone,
and transform every stumbling block
into a stepping stone.

—GAIL BROOK BURKET

8

JOYCATCHING

He who binds to himself a joy
Does the winged life destroy.
But he who kisses the joy as it flies
Lives in eternity's sun rise.

—WILLIAM BLAKE

9

LIVING IN THE MOMENT

10

From too much love of living,
From hope and fear set free,
We thank with brief thanksgiving
Whatever gods may be...

—ALGERNON CHARLES SWINBURNE

WHAT THE HEART KNOWS

11

This is what the heart knows beyond all words, if we
can find a way to listen: that beyond our small sense
of things a magnificent light surrounds us, more than
anyone could ask for. This is what prayer as gratitude
can open us to.

—MARK NEPO

HOLY, HOLY, HOLY

12

All life is one, and everything that lives is holy: plants, animals and Man. All must eat to live and nourish one another. We bless the lives that have died to give us food. Let us eat consciously, resolving by our work to pay the debt of our existence.

—JOHN G. BENNETT

GOOD WILL FOR ALL

To educate yourself for the feeling of gratitude means to take nothing for granted, but to always seek out and value the kind that will stand behind the action. Nothing that is done for you is a matter of course. Everything originates in a will for the good, which is directed at you. Train yourself never to put off the word or action for the expression of gratitude.

13

—ALBERT SCHWEITZER

THE BIGGER PICTURE

14

Two kinds of gratitude: The sudden kind we feel for
what we take; the larger kind we feel for what we give.

—EDWIN ARLINGTON ROBINSON

SEEING SILVER LININGS

15

Gratitude is medicine for a heart devastated by tragedy.
If you can only be thankful for the blue sky, then do so.

—RICHELLE E. GOODRICH

ROOTED IN GRATITUDE

16

The roots of all goodness lie in the soil of appreciation
for goodness.

—THE DALAI LAMA

BLESSING TO BLESSING

Learn to get in touch with the silence within yourself and know that everything has a purpose. There are no mistakes, no coincidences, all events are blessings given to us to learn from.

—Elisabeth Kübler-Ross

THE NEEDS OF THE MANY OUTWEIGH THE NEEDS OF THE ONE

The miracle is this—the more we share, the more we have.

—Leonard Nimoy

MAY YOU LIVE SURROUNDED BY JOY

19

May your home be filled with laughter and the warm embrace of a summer day. May you find peacefulness and beauty, challenge, and satisfaction, humor and insight, healing and renewal, love and wisdom, as in a quiet heart. May you always feel that what you have is enough.

—ANONYMOUS

THE GREAT MYSTERY

20

Life is a great and wondrous mystery, and the only thing we know that we have for sure is what is right here right now. Don't miss it.

—LEO BUSCAGLIA

GRATITUDE ADJUSTMENTS

None is more impoverished than the one who has no
gratitude. Gratitude is a currency that we can mint for
ourselves, and spend without fear of bankruptcy.

—FRED DE WITT VAN AMBURGH

PEACE IS EVERYWHERE

That is perfect. This is perfect.
Perfect comes from perfect.
Take perfect from perfect, the remainder is perfect.
May peace and peace and peace be everywhere.

—THE UPANISHADS

OPPORTUNITIES FOR APPRECIATION

Thanksgiving comes to us out of the prehistoric
dimness, universal to all ages and all faiths. At whatever
straws we must grasp, there is always a time for gratitude
and new beginnings.

—J. ROBERT MOSKIN

Gifts Come in Many Forms

24

After a good dinner one can forgive anybody, even one's own relations.

—Oscar Wilde

Lucky Is the World

Our holiday food splurge was a small crate of tangerines, which we found ridiculously thrilling after an eight-month abstinence from citrus...Lily hugged each one to her chest before undressing it as gently as a doll. Watching her do that as she sat cross-legged on the floor one morning in pink pajamas, with bliss lighting her cheeks, I thought: Lucky is the world, to receive this grateful child. Value is not made of money, but a tender balance of expectation and longing.

25

—Barbara Kingsolver

BLESSINGS ON YOUR HOUSE

For peaceful homes, and healthful days,
For all the blessings Earth displays,
We owe Thee thankfulness and praise,
Giver of all!

—CHRISTOPHER WADSWORTH, ANGLICAN BISHOP

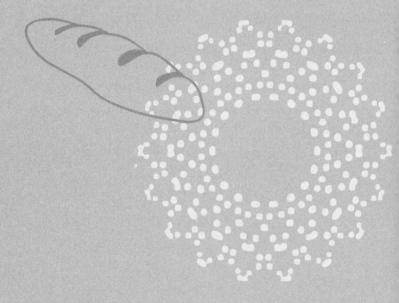

27

What other place could I have entered as innocent and helpless as this one? Where else could I find the beauty and diversity of Beings as are here on the Earth? And where else offers the challenges which, according to the Mayan calendar, include not only a total shift in this lifetime in the way humanity thinks and asks, but also a much larger shift in the whole cosmos that is almost unimaginable in its breadth and scope? Truly, we sit on the cusp of an age where anything can happen!

I don't know about you, but I feel very grateful to be here. Even when things aren't going my way, I look around and can't help but think what a beautiful place this is and how amazing it is that I get to be here at this time to unravel the wondrous mysteries of life.

—TONY BURROUGHS

It's a Beautiful World

Take one thing with another, and the world is a pretty good sort of world, and it is our duty to make the best of it, and be grateful.

—Benjamin Franklin

Two Thumbs Up!

Just do the next right thing, and be grateful for the chance you have to go do that. It's *that* simple. *Really.*

—Roger Ebert

Our Daily Prayer

30

"Thank you" is the best prayer that anyone could say. I say that one a lot. Thank you expresses extreme gratitude, humility, understanding.

—Alice Walker

This Most Wonderful Day

If we are ever to enjoy life, now is the time—not tomorrow, nor next year, nor in some future life after we have died. The best preparation for a better life 31 next year is a full, complete, harmonious, joyous life this year. Our beliefs in a rich future life are of little importance unless we coin them into a rich present life. Today should always be our most wonderful day.

—Thomas Dreier

WRITE YOUR OWN GRACE

What are your favorite words
for gratefulness?

....

....

....

....

....

ABOUT BOSS

A portion of the proceeds from *The Grateful Table* will go to Building Opportunities for Self-Sufficiency (BOSS). BOSS operates a network of housing and support services in Berkeley, Hayward, and Oakland, California. They work directly with at-risk youth and families to help them get back on their feet. BOSS's programs provide whatever level of support people need and request in order to build health, wellness, and self-sufficiency, whether they're seeking one-time assistance or help for longer periods of time.

You can donate to BOSS via their website or by mailing a check made out to BOSS. All donations are tax deductible.

Building Opportunities for Self-Sufficiency
www.self-sufficiency.org
2065 Kittredge St.
Suite E
Berkeley, CA 94704

INDEX

ABOUT THE AUTHOR

BRENDA KNIGHT grew up on a farm in Point Pleasant, West Virginia, and learned how to appreciate life from her mother, Helen. After a brief career as a high school English teacher, she began working for HarperCollins, and is now a twenty-year publishing veteran. She is also the author of the American Book Award-winning *Women of the Beat Generation*, *Rituals for Life* and *Wild Women and Books*. She is an avid gardener and seed saver, and volunteers for the American Cancer Society as a counselor for the newly diagnosed. She teaches at the San Francisco Writer's Conference and leads workshops on "Putting Your Passion on Paper." The founding editor of Viva Editions, a division of Cleis Press, Brenda lives in the San Francisco Bay Area.